THE 25% CASH MACHINE

Double Digit Income Investing

BRYAN PERRY

Foreword by Tobin Smith

BICENTENNIAL
1807
WILEY
2007
BICENTENNIAL

John Wiley & Sons, Inc.

Published by John Wiley & Sons, Inc., Hoboken, New Jersey.
Published simultaneously in Canada.

For general information on our other products and services or for technical support,
please contact our Customer Care Department within the United States at
(800) 762-2974, outside the United States at (317) 572-3993 or fax (317) 572-4002.

Wiley also publishes its books in a variety of electronic formats. Some content that
appears in print may not be available in electronic books. For more information
about Wiley products, visit our web site at www.wiley.com.

Library of Congress Cataloging-in-Publication Data:
Perry, Bryan, 1959–
  The 25% cash machine : double-digit income investing / Bryan Perry.
       p. cm.
  "Published simultaneously in Canada."
  Includes bibliographical references and index.
  ISBN-13: 978-0-470-09552-2 (cloth)
  ISBN-10: 0-470-09552-0 (cloth)
  1. Finance, Personal.   2. Investments.   I. Title.   II. Title: Twenty-
five percent cash machine.
  HG179.P3668   2007
  332.6—dc22
                                                    2006029983

Printed in the United States of America.

10 9 8 7 6 5 4 3 2 1

CONTENTS

Part Three
A New Generation of Double-Digit Income Investments

Part Four
Let's Get Started Building Your Own 25% Cash Machine

FOREWORD

Ladies and gentlemen, you are only as "rich" as you feel. And without a bulletproof foundation of income and high dividend-paying equities, you will never feel rich.

It all started with conversations with a few of my ChangeWave members who desired a strategy to make high income like clockwork. Not the 3 to 3.5 percent the "Dogs of the Dow" might pay. And certainly not 4 percent from some intermediate bond fund with no hope for capital gains.

Nope. They wanted to know—having seen many over-the-top promotions in their day—if there really was a safe way to make 10 percent yields consistently and reasonably expect nice capital gains on top of that.

Of course, I've got some experience in this area—I've helped my newsletter subscribers earn 10 to 12 percent from our energy trusts over the past few years. But I knew my colleague at ChangeWave, Bryan Perry, was the expert in our group—with 23 plus years experience running money for folks with much the same needs.

So we set Bryan loose on the project. And I guess you could say we created a monster.

The response has been overwhelming. We started with a short Special Report that explained the basics of what Bryan calls *Double-Digit Income Investing* and figured that would be it.

But we couldn't have been more wrong. Over 9,000 members of our ChangeWave family downloaded this report, from the few brief times we mentioned it.

We then talked with a number of people after this Special Report came out, and they told us that this brief introduction was a good idea.

But time and time again, we got comments and questions that all boil down pretty much like this: "Can you do more to help us get this right?"

And that's when Bryan hatched the idea for this book so that he could explain his strategy and reach hundreds of thousands—we figured the concepts might be easier to grasp this way. Plus he could detail even more investment categories, provide more cornerstone investments, and motivate you to get started.

And that's when we decided that *The 25% Cash Machine* wasn't just a short report or a brief online video seminar. It was a book that would provide the best way to help meet investors' needs.

Let me be brutally honest for a moment. Maybe you believe you've already got everything you need to make a success of double-digit income investing on your own. If so, my hat's off to you.

However, if the whole thing sounds like something you're interested in, but you're not quite sure how to make it all work correctly, I hope you'll read on. I'm going to tell you why it just might be a good idea to get some help from the guy who basically invented the 25% Cash Machine.

But there's one more reason why I want you to read this book: I hope you'll use it to take this time to get your house in order, so to speak. Trade out any of the "dead dividend stocks" we've identified for you; decide how much cash you might want to commit to this program over time; and get ready to hit the ground running.

I'm not saying you need to make all your decisions right away, of course. Sit down. Read this book. Take the time you need to be thoroughly comfortable. But the sooner you start, the sooner you'll get your own 25% Cash Machine rolling. And the sooner you'll start cashing fat checks and earning nice capital gains, month after month, for the rest of your life.

TOBIN SMITH
Founder, *ChangeWave Investing*
North Bethesda, Maryland

PREFACE

All of a sudden *income investing* has become fashionable. Brokers are recommending dividend-paying stocks again. High yield investments are becoming the talk of cocktail parties. It's dawning on people that getting paid 4 to 5 percent on CDs or money markets isn't going to get it done in today's world of investing.

Business Development Companies. Canadian Business Trusts. Closed-end funds. Convertible securities. Master Limited Partnerships. REITs. It seems as if there are more investment vehicles available today for individual investors that will generate relatively safe, high dividends.

Welcome to the World of Double-Digit Income Investing

An easy-to-understand approach that generates exceptional cash flow and can produce life-changing wealth from a diversified portfolio of freely traded securities that you can manage on your own.

Double-digit income investing is ideal for those investors who are looking to generate income from their investments and are willing to take on some risk to achieve yields that are twice as high as most other income investments.

The Low-Income, High-Inflation Dilemma

What is so different now? This form of investing is relatively new because historically when the economy rebounded, interest rates would spike way up, affording income investors the opportunity to lock in 7 to 10 percent yields on guaranteed investments like money markets and CDs during the top of each cycle.

Not so this time. Thanks to spiking energy prices and high levels of productivity, the economy is enjoying strong growth, yet not getting overheated, keeping core inflation down with interest rates that are no higher than 4.5 percent. This places income investors in a high-inflation, low-yield market as normal living expenses like housing, property taxes, home and vehicle maintenance, utilities, gasoline, medical care, education, travel and entertainment continue to spiral higher.

For income investors seeking yields from traditional vehicles like money markets, CDs, and bonds, these are frustrating times.

I personally follow 15 classes of securities that are all designed to pay out dividends around 10 percent and even more. Traditional income products like money markets, Treasury bonds, CDs, Ginny Maes (GNMAs), and utility and bank stocks are all paying no more than 5 percent. That's it.

And yet there are many Wall Street fixed-income brokers telling their clients that these are juicy yields. They would like us to believe that a 4 percent dividend is a good yield on your money that competes between bonds and stocks.

That's because we've been in such a low interest rate environment for so long that venturing out from traditional income vehicles like blue chip dividend paying stocks, CDs, bonds, and money markets into alternative investments is just not what most brokerages and banks are geared to handle.

Do you know how many 3 percent-paying big name stocks are big-time losers? A lot! After working for some of the biggest wire houses in the business, looking back, I can see how the brokerage community gets comfortable with such low-yield equity investments.

They are complacent about hunting out the great stories with the big yields and strong upside potential because the stories about many of these hybrid securities are harder to understand and harder to tell than just pitching Pfizer to their clients. Today, Pfizer is the most widely held stock in America. The white-shoe firms will tell you the stock is a safe haven, suitable for widows and orphans, right? Sure.

You just buy it and put it away . . . right. Well I don't know about you, but a 3 percent yield on my income and growth money stinks and this type of dividend strategy is a loser. Shares of Pfizer, America's most widely held stock, have fallen from $47 to $24, or −47 percent, since 2001. This story topped out in 1999 with the new bull market in generic drugs took off. The stock is hitting multiyear lows and millions of U.S. investors seem to still be in love with it. Am I missing something? Sell the pig and move on.

Like I said, the list of big-name dead money stocks is long and illustrious. Seems some investors don't mind getting crushed as long as they get their dividends in yesterday's stocks whose best years are history.

These are the kinds of 3 percent income stocks Wall Street is still pushing on their clients. Talk about getting bagged.

A New Way to Invest: High-Yield Investments

When I say "very high," I mean it. Not 4 percent money markets or 3 percent yields from tired old blue chips. I'm talking payouts that you can structure monthly, if you wish, that pay you 10 percent right away. (Some yields rise to 15 percent or more.)

One important thing to remember: I'm not pushing junk. These unique securities are all backed by strong underlying businesses. They simply differ from General Electric or Citigroup in one key way.

Rather than keep the business profits in the company's coffers to fuel extravagant lifestyles or finance another ill-fated acquisition binge, these securities are structured to "pass through" those profits to investors, like you.

If you're an income investor, you'd have to be nuts not to investigate these methods further. It's pretty simple to do, and the payoffs are SWEET.

If you're a growth investor, I reckon you could use a little more certainty—especially in times like these. Heck, I love growth stocks. But even though I'm not retired, I keep a bunch of money in these high-yield investments. I just roll my yields over and watch my wealth compound faster and faster.

That'll put a big smile on your face.

Capital Gains, Too

These double-digit income securities come with a unique advantage over most investments. There are many different types to choose from, and each type tends to shine at different points in the economic cycle. Yes, even in an economic downturn.

In fact, I expect demand to soar for many of these securities as investors grow more and more worried. Why? Two reasons.

First, it's all about yield. Investments that automatically pay you 10 percent annually look mighty attractive when the going gets rough.

And second, many of our holdings will really shine in tough times. Some do well when interest rates drop, as they would in a recession. Others do business in very boring industries, which aren't subject to big swings when the economy is hot or cold.

That's why these safe havens will attract more and more attention on every hint of bad economic news.

Over the years, I've found that 15 percent annual capital gains are the norm—a number that I see as very doable in the coming year, as well.

So when you take the 10 percent yield and tie it to the 15 percent capital gains, you get a *25% Cash Machine.*

What Do I Know about Double-Digit Income Investing?

I have a healthy passion for helping individual investors and a strong belief in income investing for my family and my goals. More important, for over 20 years I worked for some of best and brightest Wall Street firms as high-yield investing evolved from the exclusive playground for the "rich and famous" to a place where the advantage has swung to the individual investor with an online brokerage account. Here's more about me:

- I have over 20 years' experience working as a financial adviser for major Wall Street firms including Bear Sterns, Paine Webber, and Lehman Brothers.
- I've always had an affinity for high-yield investments because I was in that universe as a high-yield junk bond broker during the high-flying days of Drexel Burnham and Michael Milken.
- I worked in fixed-income securities for 10 years being privy to the inner workings of these investments—"the good, the bad and the ugly."

- I've managed money for clients for over 10 years utilizing an array of investment strategies and found double-digit income investing the consistent safe, winner year after year.
- I continue to write and edit for thousands of happy subscribers my *25% Cash Machine* newsletter discussing and recommending double-digit income investments.

My approach to high-yield investing is unique—combining in-depth fundamental research with the guidance of the ChangeWave Alliance research. And, I like taking complex investment strategies and breaking them down into easy-to-understand advice for investors.

Here's How the 25% Cash Machine Works

You'll own a basket of special-case, high-yield securities—managing them, from time to time as needed, to rotate among the strongest sectors of the economy.

You probably already know about some of these income securities—you may even have owned a couple of them. But many will be new to you—they get very little, to no, coverage in the popular press. And I can virtually guarantee that no one has ever explained why, how, and when you should own each type to maximize your returns.

This unique investing strategy stems from my 23 years of real-world experience in managing money for hundreds of demanding, and very happy, clients. So you get strategies proven, and perfected, over time, which consistently deliver around 10 percent income and 15 percent (at least) capital gains annually.

$$$ Make Money like Clockwork

If you get all your kicks from investing in the next big thing, I'm probably starting to bore you. But if you like rolling up your wealth like clockwork, there's a lot to like at the *25% Cash Machine*.

And if 10 percent annual income plus 15 percent, or more, in capital gains sounds like a good addition to your investing strategy, then get ready to enjoy a great ride through a brave new world of double-digit income investments.

Introduction

I've been investing and trading other people's money since 1984, when I started as a broker-trainee at the Wall Street firm of Smith Barney. Remember those John Houseman commercials? "We make money the old fashioned way, we eeaarrrnnn it." Well, after many years of managing assets of almost every risk level and style, I finally realized it was possible to realistically beat the S&P 500 every year, while also providing clients with an extraordinarily high-dividend yield on their money. This realization didn't just strike me one day as I sat around pondering new strategies. What caused me to recognize what's possible to investors was born of tragedy.

I have a good friend named Caren whose husband died suddenly in early 2002, leaving this 36-year-old mother of three without the primary income from a very successful real estate brokerage business. To take proper care of her family, people advised Caren to get a job and just outsource the kids after school. After all, that's the most logical step in a normal world.

Well, for Caren, her world was anything but normal. She didn't want to get a job and leave her kids to be raised by somebody else. It's not that she couldn't have found a good job, or didn't want to work. On the contrary, Caren is a very intelligent, do-whatever-it-takes kind of person who was fully prepared to make the tough decisions after her husband's sudden passing. The prevailing issue in Caren's life is that one of her children is autistic and must be monitored at all times. For those of you who know anything about caring for an autistic child, you know it's a full-time job that can completely wear out even the strongest of two-parent families. So consider how difficult the task would be for a single parent who also has to work full-time, and who also has to take care of two other children. Being away from her family 50 hours a week just wasn't an option for Caren.

Fortunately, Caren's husband had the foresight to have purchased a life insurance policy that paid a lump sum of $400,000. Caren's goal was to put that money to work so she could live off of it until she figured out how to structure her life going forward. To help her figure out the best way to put that life insurance money to work, Caren consulted the treasurer of the church we both attend. Knowing that I was in the profession of managing assets, the treasurer contacted me to see if I had any advice that could help Caren figure out her situation.

The treasurer told Caren about the return on assets she could expect from traditional income investments like money markets, CDs, Treasuries, or mortgage-backed securities. After hearing about the approximate 5 percent return her money would generate, Caren immediately knew that she wouldn't be able to live on that level of income without selling her home and moving away from her vital support system of close friends and family. Getting 5 percent on $400,000 was only going to generate $20,000 per year, or about $1,650 per month. That just wasn't going to get it done.

Caren really wanted to take a course of action that would allow her to hold on to her home. She knew that if she wanted to generate more income per month from that $400,000, she would have to do something with her money other than just buying CDs or bonds. She also knew that getting a better return involved more risk than these guaranteed investments, but it was a risk she was willing to take.

In preparing for my meeting with Caren, I researched every available class of security I knew of for the highest dividend or bond yields available. I knew that trying to meet income needs by trading the market or relying on some exotic covered call strategy was going to involve too much risk and way too much turnover within her portfolio. The sum of my research resulted in my designing an income portfolio of stocks that paid out an aggregate yield of 10 percent. I presented my findings to Caren, and told her about my strategy for generating the income she needed. Apparently I made a good impression on her because in July 2002 she gave me the go-ahead to start investing her money.

I positioned her $400,000 insurance money into what is presently known as my "strategic high-income portfolio." With a yield of 10 percent less my management fee of 1 percent, Caren's account would generate annual income of $36,000 per year, representing a 9 percent current yield on her money. That would translate into monthly income of $3,000 per month—almost double that of what she was going to get from conventional fixed income investments.

Caren was still due some follow-on residual sales commissions from her husband's real estate business, so she elected to take out only $2,500 per month in income. She then had me reinvest the remaining portion of her monthly dividends to try and compound the growth of the principal. I then spread the money out among 40 stocks, putting $10,000 in each stock so that no single holding represented more than 2.5 percent weighting of the total portfolio.

Today, Caren's account is worth $500,000 and it's yielding 11.5 percent. That's cash flow of $57,500 per year. I am proud to say that she is now receiving a monthly check of $4,300 per month. Caren is what I call my "poster child" success story, and I love to share her tale of triumph with everybody.

Another success story I like to share illustrates how my strategic high-income strategy can serve very real client needs. Dr. Jones, a retired physician from Southern California, has been a long-standing subscriber to ChangeWave Research. He has attended most of the trade shows that I have spoken at over the past five years.

During one of my workshops, he heard about what I had done for Caren, and he approached me after my talk about his own circumstance. His terminally ill sister required in-home nursing care that he was paying for out of his own pocket. Initially, Dr. Jones opened an account with me in his sister's name with a deposit of $200,000 as a way to set up an incremental income stream for future nursing care expenses.

We started back in March 2004, and Dr. Jones instructed me to initially reinvest all the dividend and interest income until the cost of daily nursing care rose to a level where a monthly withdrawal would be necessary to pay for the added expenditures. Fortunately, 2004 was an especially good year for strategic high-income investing, as well as for the market in general. By year's end, the value of that $200,000 had grown to $235,000—a return of 17 percent over just seven months.

At Dr. Jones' request, I merged that account with another account valued at $50,000, bringing the new combined account total to $285,000 by mid-2005. In a very short time, this account grew to $300,000. Then, in September 2005, Dr. Jones requested that I start sending him a monthly payment of $2,500. His sister's condition had worsened, and she now required round-the-clock nursing care. This was the very thing we set his account up for, and when the time came, Dr. Jones was financially prepared.

Sending out $2,500 per month meant extracting $30,000 a year from the account, or 10 percent of the value of the underlying assets. Fortunately, the portfolio I put together was yielding over 11 percent per year—more than enough to cover the monthly payments and my 1 percent management fee. Once again, my style of high-yield investing provided a wonderful solution to a problem that I'm sure many of you face right now, and that's making sure you have enough income to deal with life's challenges.

The main reason why I wrote this book is to show you the possibilities of strategic high-income investing. Whether you need to create income from a one-time life insurance payment, provide for out-of-pocket medical expenses, pay for college tuition, generate extra income in order to afford the house payment after retirement, or simply to enhance your present income so as to be able to buy that new car, strategic high-income investing can and will work for you.

Right now we are in what I call a high-inflation, low-yield environment. This situation constitutes a major problem for those of us who simply need more bang for our investment buck than traditional financial instruments offer. To achieve many of the financial goals we've set for ourselves, we will have to put our money to work in new, creative ways.

I'm here to tell you that my strategic high-income strategy can help you achieve your income-generating goals. The nuts and bolts of this strategy form the basis for what I'm presenting in this short and hopefully insightful read. It is my objective to show the world how strategic high-income investing can help investors take charge of their income-generation assets, and achieve higher returns than would otherwise be unattainable in the conventional world of fixed income investing.

In the time it takes to fly from the East Coast to the West Coast and back, you'll learn what makes this successful strategy tick, and why it has worked throughout the various market conditions of the past five years. You'll also learn that there's a viable portfolio management solution to traditional low-income returns that not only delivers double-digit yields, but that also has the ability to achieve 10 to 20 percent annual growth on your principal.

A lot has happened in the securities market since 1984 when I first entered the business. We now have huge opportunities that never existed before to manage our income properly. There are a plethora of new and evolutionary products that have come to the market during the past decade, and these products have opened up a world of opportunity for income investors. These new products, employed with a sound and proven strategy born of the need to solve real-world problems, can help you get more from your money than you ever thought possible. My hope is that with the knowledge you glean from these pages, you'll be able to build your own 25% Cash Machine.

1

Welcome to the New World of Income Investing

What is my favorite day of the month? The 15th, of course. That's the day I get my dividend check from my favorite high-income stocks and funds.

You see, for years now, I have quietly developed a 25% Cash Machine strategy managing money for many satisfied clients. I've used this simple, but tried-and-true approach to generate hefty monthly income (usually on the 15th of the month) and market-beating gains at the same time.

I've been working to help regular people like you and me with this incredible income opportunity for some time now. Month after month they roll their dividends and cash distributions into more and more shares and units of investment, and grow richer every week, inch by inch.

And, these 10 to 12 percent dividend payers are growing steadily at the same time—their money's been compounding at the rate of 15 percent per year.

A 25% Cash Machine! It's time to share the secret with you.

A 25% Cash Machine: Double-Digit Income Investing

Welcome to the world of double-digit income investing, a methodical approach to providing income investors with detailed high-yield strategies that generate exceptional cash flow and produce long-term capital appreciation from a diversified portfolio of several classes of freely traded securities by way of dynamic sector rotation.

Let me begin by stating just how successful this investment strategy really is. I've been investing money for people as an asset manager for more than 20 years. And after having tried just about every investment approach to enhancing the value of long-term portfolios, there is no other method I've applied that consistently beats the market's historical returns year after year, pays a whopping yield and exhibits less volatility than a portfolio of blue-chip stocks.

Double-digit income investing is simple: Own and manage a basket of about 20 to 25 high-yield securities and rotate among the strongest sectors of the economy.

In this book, *The 25% Cash Machine,* you will learn how double-digit income investing holds many of the attributes today's income and growth investors are looking for:

- It is highly diversified.
- It is flexible in its strategy.
- It pays a whopping yield.
- It is highly liquid.
- It offers upside appreciation with less volatility than that of common stocks.

How sweet is that?

This is why I wrote *The 25% Cash Machine,* to show you how to get maximum cash flow out of your income assets while benefiting from meaningful capital appreciation as well.

The Current Low-Income Dilemma

Soaring energy prices have slowed spending and the growth of core inflation. Therefore, bond yields remain low even though the cost of living in the form of housing, food, gas, education, and everyday services has risen dramatically.

Talk about the mother of all conundrums! Household expenses are gapping higher and we've got a bond market that's topping out at 4.5 percent on the 30-year Treasury with the best-performing blue-chip stocks maybe paying out about a 2.5 to 3 percent yield.

Wall Street would like us to believe that a 3 percent dividend is a good yield on your money. Why? Because we've been in such a low interest rate environment for so long that venturing out from traditional income vehicles like blue-chip dividend paying stocks, CDs, bonds, and money markets into alternative investments is just not what most brokerages and banks are geared to handle.

Do you know how many 3 percent-paying big-name stocks are big-time losers? A lot! After working for some of the biggest wire houses in the business, looking back, I can see how the brokerage community gets comfortable with such low-yield equity investments.

To face life in an environment where traditional income investments like CDs, money markets, and bonds produce only 4 to 5 percent is depressing. Nobody wants to cut short their dreams just because yields are ridiculously low.

Having independent control of our investment assets with a solid game plan is what you and I want.

And after literally trying every method of generating high monthly income from stocks and options known to man, after 20 years, at the end of the day . . . the 25% Cash Machine high-yield strategy is the total solution to beating the averages every year . . . with lower volatility, and while generating annual cash flow of 10 percent while you watch your assets appreciate.

Thousands of your fellow investors are already much richer because of one simple thing: They have begun to follow this plan.

You can enjoy a much richer retirement too, with a stream of income so generous you'll pinch yourself to see if you're dreaming.

What Is so Different about Double-Digit Income Investing?

Today, the market is ripe with hundreds of hybrid securities paying whopping yields, some in excess of 15 percent, that are backed by companies in industries that are enjoying bull market conditions. This approach to double-digit income investing is ideal for any investor looking at fixed income investments like CDs, money markets, and bonds, whether the goal is to generate cash for spending, pay college tuition expenses, or finance a dream retirement.

I hear this all the time, "Sure Bryan, I can live on 4 percent, but I don't want to. I want to enjoy my retirement and I'm willing to take some risk to generate more income."

Then the 25% Cash Machine strategy is for you, my friend.

Building a dynamic portfolio of publicly traded liquid assets that throw off a 10 percent stream of cash belongs right in that base 50 to 60 percent of the investment pyramid. We call these high-yield equity investments *bond equivalents,* which simply means they are alternative forms of income other than bonds.

Simply put, these securities are too good to pass up. I fondly recall convincing a retired pal of mine to build a nice portfolio of these stocks a few years ago. He now sits on more than $2 million and has more monthly income than he knows what to do with.

More income than he knows what to do with! SWEET!

The 25% Cash Machine Mission

If there was a mission statement for the 25% Cash Machine, it would be to show the income investor a way to beat the historical returns of the major averages, and get at least twice the dividend stream on income assets compared to what the banks and traditional blue-chip stocks are paying.

Today there are investment opportunities in virtually every sector of the market, and with the broad issuance of new income derivatives over the past 10 years, investors can literally have their cake (double-digit income) and eat it, too (capital appreciation).

The investment objective of the 25% Cash Machine is simple enough for just about anyone to understand. It is to achieve high-yield income and long-term growth through a diversified portfolio of several freely traded asset classes.

Playing the Double-Digit Income Investing Game

This book analyzes and guides you through the ins and outs of double-digit investing. The strategies laid out here will act as a foundation for building a high-income portfolio and will make it easier to manage your 25% Cash Machine.

You can't and shouldn't fund your double-digit income portfolio overnight. By following some of the very simple steps I'm about to discuss in this book, you can begin to realize double-digit dividends right away as you "craft" your high-income portfolio.

The approach you are going to read about in this book is about building a double-digit income portfolio with the idea that you will eventually own up to 25 securities.

I help you through this and talk about the hundreds of income investment opportunities available and narrow them down to a core group of recommendations you can start adding to your portfolio.

Realistic Expectations

This strategy is not meant to be a trading account. We're not looking to book short-term gains in 30, 60, or 90 days from now; quite the opposite.

You should be hoping to hold each position for years to come, resulting in steady appreciation and high income. Don't expect these stocks to trade like pure growth stocks. Sure they will move up to some degree on favorable news, but not like common stocks that retain all their earnings.

However, because of the double-digit yields these stocks pay, they don't get sold down harshly on bad news. The high-dividend yield acts like a safety net, keeping the stocks trading in a very tight range, but trending higher as well.

Know Your Objectives

We're in this game to generate a 10 to 12 percent stream of income from dividends and interest, while getting an additional 15 percent capital appreciation over time—a long time.

This is your income portfolio, something that you should build and keep for the rest of your life. We will not get 25 percent every year on our money, but over time, this approach will generate 25 percent annual "total return." Some years, we'll get more, some we'll get less.

Highly Focused Portfolio

We aren't in the mutual fund business where the fund manager buys 200 different positions for the fund, employing huge diversification. You will build a high-income portfolio of about 25 stocks (give or take a few).

I believe in some concentration, but not like holding only five to seven stocks. We have to manage the potential downside and that is why I don't like to have any single position that is over 5 percent of the total portfolio. A 5 percent position is large enough in that a stock that is working well will have plenty of impact on the overall portfolio. And a 5 percent position is small enough that if a position goes against us, it doesn't blow up the total return for the whole year.

Diversification is a key part of this strategy, but if we are too diversified, then the real winners in the portfolio have a lesser effect on the total return. Plus, without a staff of assistance helping you out, it's hard to cover more than 20 to 25 companies effectively without chewing up all of your time. So we're seeking a balance of focus and diversification to achieve the highest yield and total return.

Sector Rotation

Success from the 25% Cash Machine comes from moving your money aggressively into the right sectors as business conditions favor them. This is not a static portfolio, it is a dynamic portfolio.

Yes, I want you to hold all your stocks for years to come, but they aren't guaranteed securities. They're income securities based on operating enterprises paying big dividends because of bullish business conditions.

If for some reason the economy shows clear signs of recessionary pressures, it would be time to rotate out of oil and gas income stocks and into things like mortgage REITs, healthcare REITs, high-yield preferred stocks, corporate bonds, and other deflationary sensitive sectors.

There will be times when you will sell investments and re-invest those funds in another sector.

Patience

These income investments don't move around like common stocks, but there is some degree of volatility and you can definitely save a point here and there if you buy the pullbacks accordingly. Build your portfolio carefully. I call it "crafting" a portfolio. Get the feel for this approach to income investing because it will build your confidence.

However, if the volatility is too much to deal with or losses too hard to bear, then maybe this approach isn't for you. It's all about risk/reward ratios. And in the case of this strategy, I believe the reward is well worth the risk, as long as the risk is managed properly.

Have Some Fun

You now have my permission to enjoy this approach, follow it, and have fun with it. Once you get to fully acquainted with the double-digit income investing approach, I believe you will find it to be one of the most endearing components of your financial estate.

Don't try to compare this style of investing with growth stock investing. That's not what my mission and task is here. We are out to beat the bank by twice what they are paying at all times. If the banks are paying 5 percent, we want to pay at least 10 percent. If the banks are paying 7.5 percent on CDs, your double-digit income portfolio should be kicking out at least a 15 percent yield. If not, why take the risk?

Listen, I have taken enough risk in the past 23 years to know what and what doesn't work on a long-term basis. Learn from those that have made all the mistakes, including me. Investing is a multiyear process.

Unless you want to be a day trader, this form of income and growth investing is the best model I know of that consistently performs well year after year.

If This Is Too Easy, Then Buy a Car Dealership

Why do you think rich guys want to own car dealerships? Yeah, part of it is ego, maybe a big part. However, as a rule of thumb, car dealerships have spun off an average of 13 percent cash flow since the car dealership system began. The only problem is that it costs $10 million to buy a Honda dealership. Dang! I knew there was a catch.

Think about what you would be doing with $10 million in cash if you had it. Would you invest in stocks that pay big dividends or would you invest in privately owned businesses that throw off massive cash flow? Well, take comfort in knowing that many folks that do have that kind of money with the freedom of making those choices do, in fact, choose to invest in high-yield stocks instead of private businesses. Why? They simply don't want the hassle of running a business. Professional management is a beautiful thing. When you have the money, freedom of your time becomes the prize.

What I am trying to do with all that I know and with all that I have learned in my 23 years of professional investing is to identify those businesses that you would otherwise buy for yourself on a private basis, yet that trade as public securities. I don't consider what I do speculation, not after what I've been through. And I seriously don't think you want to hear my personal Wall Street tales of life at big brokerage firms. Books like that have already been written numerous times.

I consider what I bring to you in this book a path for immediate return on your invested capital and a path of least resistance to long-term growth and the security of being invested in strong cash flow–oriented businesses that trade like water. Why not learn from me? I have been tested by fire, and that includes the crash of 1987, the junk bond meltdown of 1994, and dealing with the carnage from the Internet bubble days of 2000.

It takes a certain attitude to know how to read the markets and react properly. Not to be too soldier of fortune–like, but in the Marines, when you check in at Parris Island, South Carolina, for basic training, they break you down, and then they build you up. How do I know that? One of my best friends and ushers in my wedding 21 years ago was the fastest-rising Sergeant in modern Marine Corps history because of an unwavering discipline of knowing when to invest in certain people and when not to.

Investing is a lot like obtaining a Marine Corps-like discipline. I personally speak with each and every entity that I invest in, for myself and for the benefit of my clients. I have a litany of questions that I have established over the years that pretty much tells me whether or not I want to consider putting hard-earned capital behind the CEO or CFO and the company or entity they represent.

I'll know in the very early going whether or not I'm speaking with a winner or some kind of wannabe. That kind of knowledge only comes with experience and intuition.

I think once you do this kind of investing for a while; you will come to appreciate just what it is I'm talking about. This is the oasis of investing folks. Come along, take a cool drink, and rest in the knowledge that you have placed your money in a time-tested investment model for today's income investor.

Now let's see how everything all works.

PART ONE

THE PROBLEM: LOW INCOME IN A HIGH-INFLATION WORLD

2

The Low-Inflation Myth

Have you noticed that over the past few years, things just cost more? I know I've noticed it, and I'm quite sure that all of you have as well. In fact, $100 worth of goods and services purchased at the turn of the twenty-first century would cost you about $118 in 2006. That's an 18 percent increase in the overall cost of goods and services in just six years. I don't know about you, but I doubt most of us were fortunate enough to see our personal incomes rise 18 percent over that same time period.

Yet, if you listen to economists, bankers, and politicians talk about the rising cost of living, you would think that all was quiet on the inflation front. But how can that be? I mean, we all know from personal experience that we are paying more now to fill our gas tanks, heat our homes, feed our families and send the kids to school. We are all feeling the pain of these increasing costs every time we stop at the pump, write checks to the utility companies or return from a trip to the grocery store. So why do we keep hearing that costs aren't increasing any faster than they have in the past?

Well, the reason why the powers that be can perpetrate what I call the "low-inflation myth," is due to a little selective reading of the overall picture on inflation. The line here goes something like this: On an historical basis, aggregate consumer price increases are generally in line with the average rate of inflation since about 1980.

Historically speaking, this perfunctory reading of inflation can be considered statistically accurate. However, as the great British statesman Benjamin Disraeli was once alleged to have said, "There are three kinds of lies: lies, damned lies and statistics." So, does this mean I am calling those who claim we are in a low-inflation environment liars? You bet I am. Because by focusing on just the aggregate statistics, those who say we are in a low-inflation environment are in effect painting a much prettier picture of reality than what we see around us everyday.

My definition of inflation is not just relegated to the overall rate of inflation as measured by the Consumer Price Index (CPI). My definition of inflation is a little more up close and personal than just the data put out by a bunch of number crunchers in Washington. I have what I consider a personal relationship with inflation because the rising cost of the things I normally buy directly affects my overall purchasing power—and my overall quality of life.

I suspect you also have your own personal relationship with inflation that affects the decisions you are forced to make in your lives. It's the finite nature of all resources that compel us into making choices with our dollars, and try as we may, there is simply no escaping the economic principle of scarcity. As a consumer, wage earner, or investor, there is just no getting around the increasing costs of purchasing the things we need.

Statistics—Telling a Tainted Story

Most of us have heard the term CPI bandied about by economist, bankers, investment professionals and commentators in the financial news media, but for those of you who don't know what CPI actually refers to, it is basically just a measure of the changes in prices charged for consumer goods and services. The overall CPI number is commonly used as an indication of the rate of inflation in the U.S. economy. This measure of inflation is also used to estimate the increase in the cost of living. CPI data is compiled and calculated monthly by the Bureau of Labor Statistics (BLS), a division of the U.S. Department of Labor.

Let's take a look at some of the statistical data that give rise to the low-inflation myth. Table 2.1 shows us the overall CPI number for each

Table 2.1
CPI Data, 1980–2006

Year	Annual Average	Annual Percent Change (Rate of Inflation)
1980	82.4	13.5
1981	90.9	10.3
1982	96.5	6.2
1983	99.6	3.2
1984	103.9	4.3
1985	107.6	3.6
1986	109.6	1.9
1987	113.6	3.6
1988	118.3	4.1
1989	124.0	4.8
1990	130.7	5.4
1991	136.2	4.2
1992	140.3	3.0
1993	144.5	3.0
1994	148.2	2.6
1995	152.4	2.8
1996	156.9	2.9
1997	160.5	2.3
1998	163.0	1.6
1999	166.6	2.2
2000	172.2	3.4
2001	177.0	2.8
2002	179.9	1.6
2003	184.0	2.3
2004	188.9	2.7
2005	195.3	3.4
2006*	202.5	3.7

Source: Bureau of Labor Statistics.
*An estimate for 2006 is based on the change in the CPI from fourth quarter 2004 to fourth quarter 2005.

year since 1980. It also shows the annual percent change in the CPI figure, which is the key number when you hear people refer to the rate of inflation.

In 1980, the inflation rate hit 13.5 percent. That's the highest rate that we'd seen since just after World War II. I can remember those years in the early 1980s quite well. We had a stagnant economy and double-digit inflation. The so-called Misery Index (unemployment rate + inflation rate) was at its peak, and the economy was in very bad shape.

The following year we saw the rate of inflation begin to cool. Although still very high at just over the double-digit mark, inflation was substantially lower than the disastrous inaugural year of the "decade of greed." Since 1982, the rate of inflation has been in the mid-to-low single digits. Even including those sky-high years of 1980 and 1981, the average rate of overall rate of inflation since has been just under 4 percent.

Fast-forward to the twenty-first century and you'll see that based on overall CPI data during those years, we are in what can understandably be termed a relatively low-inflation environment. The average rate of inflation between 2003 and 2006 was just over 3 percent. That's much lower than the average when you include the peak inflation year of 1980 in your calculation.

Here we see the gist of the logic that created the low-inflation myth so many "experts" have been touting in recent years. I mean, even a casual observer of the data must come to the conclusion that inflation is low by historical standards, right? Well, not so fast.

The Actual Cost of the Things We Buy

Whenever I hear someone say that inflation is under control and at historically low rates, I ask them if they've found themselves paying noticeably more money these past few years for the things they use most. Nearly always the answer is an emphatic "yes." Things do cost more—a lot more. How much more? Well, it certainly seems like the cost of living has increased a great deal more than what those negligible CPI numbers the low-inflation environment proponents are always talking about. The increasing costs that you, I, and all of us have to contend with are no figment of the imagination. They are very real, and they are having a very real impact on our discretionary income.

You see, neither the modest increase in the overall CPI figure, nor the diminished purchasing power of our dollars that we talked about at the outset of this chapter begin to tell the whole story when it comes to inflation. To find out why we have to reach way down deep into our pockets just to get the things we need, we'll have to look a little deeper into the CPI data. However, I warn you that what you are about to see isn't pretty. In fact, the view from the inside the CPI can get downright ugly.

Let's take a look at some of the data from various sectors of the economy over the three-year period from April 2003 through April 2006. Figure 2.1 shows the rate of growth in the energy component that makes up a portion of the overall CPI. As you can clearly see, energy costs soared over this time period. I don't mean costs have risen just a bit more than the overall CPI, I mean they have jumped into the stratosphere.

The increase in the cost of energy was 44.55 percent. Now, you can correct me if I'm wrong, but 44.55 percent is a lot higher than the rate of

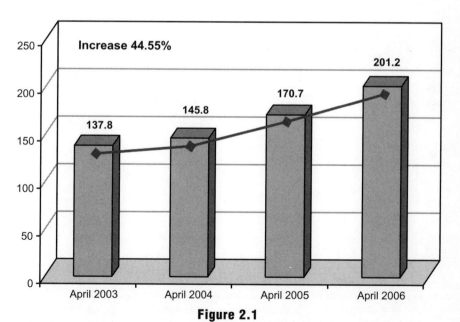

Figure 2.1
U.S. Consumer Price Index Data for Energy (Seasonally Adjusted)

inflation that those overall CPI numbers suggests. The surge in energy costs in recent years has had a pernicious effect on nearly every industry imaginable.

It costs more to power our homes, our factories, our cities, our states, and our country as a whole. There is virtually no segment of the economy immune from the rising costs of energy, and the sharp increase in this sector alone is enough to start making you think about twice about that low-inflation environment. When you have to pay more for energy, you'll have to pay more for everything that it takes energy to produce—and there isn't much out there that doesn't take energy to produce and/or transport.

A related subsector of the CPI is energy commodities. These are the raw materials that go into creating the power that we all consume. Between April 2003 and April 2006, this segment of the consumer price calculation was up 67.99 percent. Here again, a huge increase in the cost of a group of goods that the entire country needs to literally survive each day, as shown in Figure 2.2.

Figure 2.3 shows us the big one—the most high-profile example of a cost that affects everyone's bottom line nearly everyday. Yes, it's the

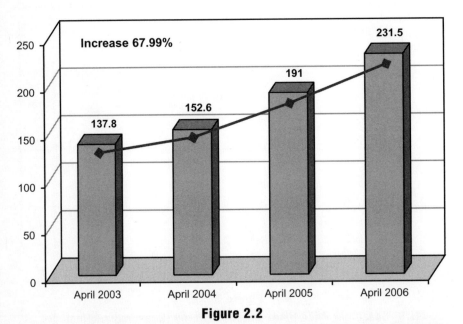

Figure 2.2

U.S. Consumer Price Index for Energy Commodities (Seasonally Adjusted)

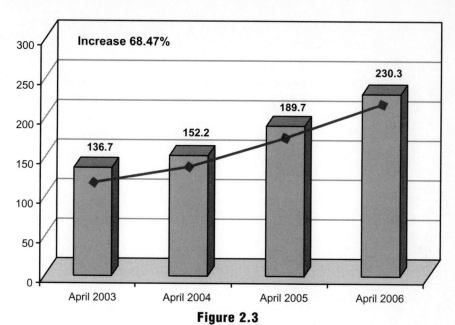

Figure 2.3
U.S. Consumer Price Index Data for Motor Fuel (Seasonally Adjusted)

cost of motor fuel, and its increase over the same three-year period is once again staggering. In just 36 months, the cost of motor fuel plowed its way higher by 68.47 percent. Think about that for a moment. What once cost consumers $30 at the pump climbed to nearly $51 in just three years. And where does this cost to you come from? It comes straight out of your household budget, and it takes a significant bite out of your overall discretionary income. If you are trying to survive on the returns provided by traditional fixed-income portfolios, the increasing cost of gasoline can really hurt.

There are many other examples of rising costs in the energy subsectors of the CPI measure. The index for gas (piped) and electricity rose a seasonally adjusted 24.5 percent from April 2003 to April 2006, as shown in Figure 2.4. The cost of natural gas services jumped 30.29 percent during that same period. Hey, when it comes to energy, I don't think there are too many people out there telling you that we are in a low-inflation environment. When it comes to energy, the low-inflation myth has just been busted.

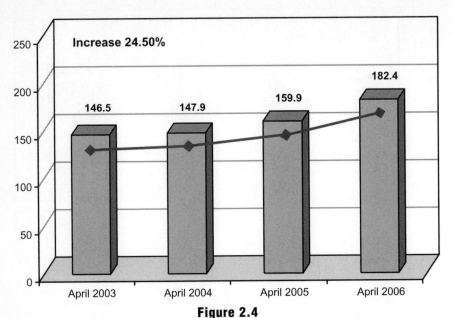

Figure 2.4
U.S. Consumer Price Index Data for Gas (Piped) and Electricity
(Seasonally Adjusted)

Housing: The Cost of Keeping That Roof

Okay, we've already seen how energy costs are digging into our bottom lines, but what about the cost of housing? Many of us have benefited a great deal from rising real estate prices these past few years, but the increase in home values also has a downside, and that is the rising cost of housing as measured by the CPI.

Figure 2.5 shows inflation in the housing sector. During our chosen three-year period, housing costs rose 9.5 percent. That may not seem like much of an increase compared to the big percentage jumps we've had in energy, but you have to consider that the cost of housing is a big-ticket item, and the biggest expense most of us will ever have. Unless you own your home outright, the increased cost of buying a new home or renting a home can wear down your personal income in a big hurry, as indicated in Figure 2.6. Again, the rising rate of inflation in the housing sector means another strike against the so-called low-inflation environment that we are supposedly steeped in.

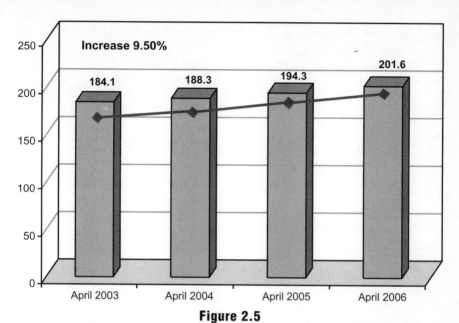

Figure 2.5
U.S. Consumer Price Index Data for Housing (Seasonally Adjusted)

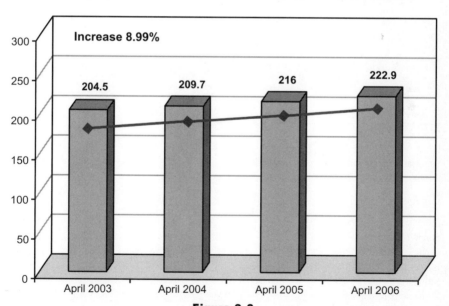

Figure 2.6
Consumer Price Index Data for Rent of Primary Residence
(Seasonally Adjusted)

Food: Everyone's Got to Eat

I know it's self-evident, but we all have to consume food each day to continue on as living beings. Food is not something we can do without, nor would most of us ever want to do without it. And given the fact that we all must eat to live, we must also all spend money in support of our eating habit.

So what happens when the cost of food increases substantially? Well, I wish I could say we all do the prudent thing for both our pocketbooks and our waistlines and start cutting down on the amount of food we consume. Unfortunately, we humans like to eat what we like, in the quantities that we like. If we have to pay more for that privilege, then we just end up digging a little deeper into our pockets.

Table 2.2 is the American Farm Bureau's Marketbasket Survey of prices from the first quarter of 2003 to the first quarter of 2006. The key column to look at here is the one that shows the percentage change in the cost of these food stuffs over this three-year period. As you can see, every item in the Marketbasket Survey is higher. The lowest increase we

Table 2.2
American Farm Bureau Marketbasket Survey

Item	Quarter 2003 (U.S. Dollars)	Quarter 2006 (U.S. Dollars)	Change (%)
Ground chuck (1 pound)	2.10	2.84	+35
White bread (20-ounce loaf)	1.32	1.43	+8
Cheerios/Toasted oat cereal (10-ounce box)	2.78	2.89	+4
Apples (1 pound)	1.05	1.10	+5
Whole fryers (1 pound)	1.05	1.23	+17
Pork chops (1 pound)	3.10	3.39	+9
Cheddar cheese (1 pound)	3.30	3.89	+21
Bacon (1 pound)	2.91	3.09	+6
Mayonnaise (32-ounce jar)	3.14	3.28	+4
Russet potatoes (5-pound bag)	1.89	2.24	+19
Sirloin tip roast (1 pound)	3.21	3.85	+20
Whole milk (1 gallon)	2.80	3.16	+13
Vegetable oil (32-ounce bottle)	2.25	2.61	+16
All-purpose flour (5-pound bag)	1.53	1.73	+13
Corn oil (32-ounce bottle)	2.41	2.92	+21

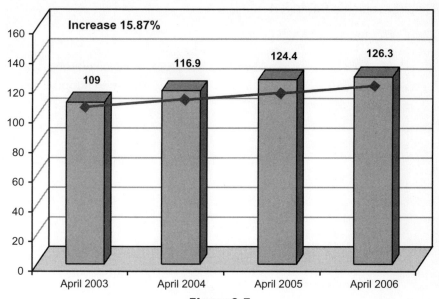

Figure 2.7
Consumer Price Index Data for Milk (Not Seasonally Adjusted)

see is 4 percent, with the highest increase seen in the price of beef, which was up 35 percent in three years.

Given the typical American diet—replete in good old-fashioned hamburgers—you've got to assume that the increased prices for beef, and grocery prices as a whole, took their toll on our overall out-of-pocket expenses. It's just another example of how inflation in the most essential of items we use daily has translated into an increase in costs that aren't readily reflected in the overall CPI number.

Here are a couple of other examples of the increasing cost of food products that almost all of us use on a daily basis: milk and coffee (Figures 2.7 and 2.8). Sorry all of you Starbucks Venti, double-shot, nonfat-milk latte lovers out there, these next couple of charts are aimed at you.

Other Goodies to Consider

It's not just the basics like energy, housing, and food that have seen their rate of inflation jump in recent years. The rising costs of other

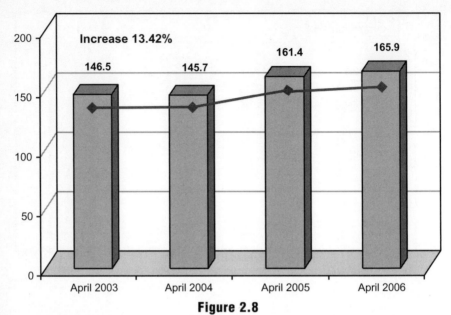

Figure 2.8
U.S. Consumer Price Index Data for Coffee (Not Seasonally Adjusted)

items many of us consider essential have also risen in the past three years. For example, how about the 20.86 percent increase in the cost of education, as indicated in Figure 2.9? What about the 13.6 percent increase in medical costs, and its corollary, an 11.71 percent jump in prescription drugs and medical supplies, as shown in Figures 2.10 and 2.11? All of these are not quite as important as energy, housing, and food, but I'd venture a guess and say that one or more of these issues are indeed very relevant to you.

How about living it up a little? Well, there too, the rate of inflation is much higher than overall CPI number reveals. The cost of lodging away from home, including hotels and motels rose 17.09 percent in our three-year sample—so much for those frequent weekend getaways. Have a pet? Well, sorry, the cost of keeping Fido also jumped relative to the overall CPI number, with the cost of pet and veterinary services clawing their way 16.14 percent higher from April 2003 to April 2006.

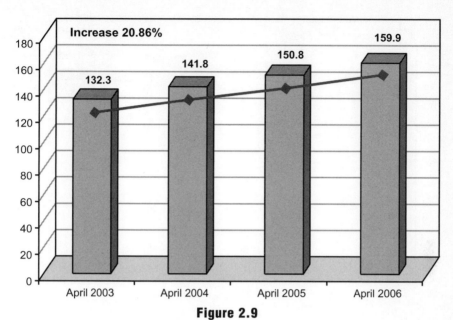

Figure 2.9
U.S. Consumer Price Index Data for Education (Seasonally Adjusted)

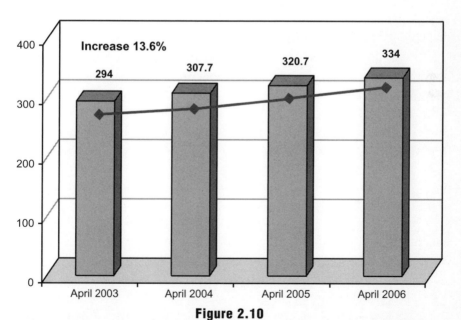

Figure 2.10
U.S. Consumer Price Index Data for Medical Care (Seasonally Adjusted)

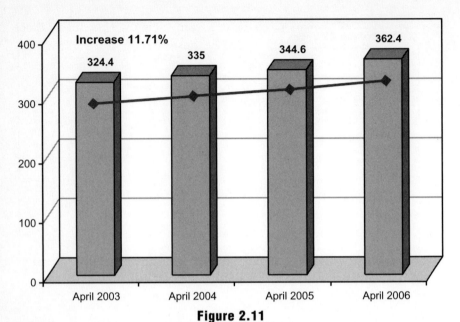

Figure 2.11
U.S. Consumer Price Index Data for Prescription Drugs and Medical Supplies (Seasonally Adjusted)

Excluding Food and Energy

Don't you just love it when you hear that the so-called "core inflation" number has come out, and that number is said to be relatively tame? Well, this is another component of the low-inflation myth that I want to quickly dispatch.

You see, when analysts use the core inflation number to measure the rate of price changes, they are using a number that excludes the often volatile food and energy sectors. But as we've already discussed, these are the sectors that we all use the most—and that have risen substantially more over the past several years compared to the overall measure of inflation. Hey, I say you can't do without food and energy, so don't leave them out of your inflation matrix.

Wrap Up

We've talked a lot about prices from April 2003 to April 2006, and you might be asking yourself why did I choose to examine prices over this time period? Well, because borrowing from their own premises, these years are prime examples of what some describe as a low-inflation environment. As we've already seen, the cost of many of the things we need—energy, food, housing—have been anything but lower over the past few years. But technically speaking, economists and politicians can still claim that by historical comparison, we are currently in a low-inflation environment.

While this claim may sound good when offered up as evidence of sound financial stewardship of the economy, those of us who have to go out and hand over the cash to pay for all of this stuff know that reality is a totally different story. We know that things cost more, and we know that our pocketbooks are just that much lighter because of it. If this is a low-inflation environment, I'd hate to see what things are going to cost in a high-inflation environment.

The point here is that even though by historical measures, overall inflation as measured by the entire CPI is rightly said to be contained, we all know that the reality of the situation in our daily lives is quite different. This is what I call the low-inflation myth, and like most myths, it can end up teaching you something about life. In this case, the message is clear. Statistics tell one story, and reality reveals a completely different tale.

The logical question to ask now is: Given the increased costs of the things we buy, how are we going to keep paying for these things without eventually feeling the tug in our wallets? How are we going to keep paying our way, living the lives we want to lead, taking care of ourselves, our spouses, our children or grandchildren, and making our lives free from the worries associated with financial shortfalls?

Well, I can tell you one way you are not going to get it done, and that is by using the traditional asset classes we've all been told are the bedrocks of a proper income portfolio. These instruments are falling woefully short of any kind of meaningful return, and in Chapter 3, you'll see exactly what I mean.

Healthy Considerations

According to the Centers for Medicare and Medicaid Services (CMS), total healthcare expenditures for 2006 are estimated to be $2.16 trillion in

*2006. That number is projected to climb to $4 trillion by 2015. Per person
health spending in 2006 will be estimated at over $7,000, and that num-
ber is expected to increase to over $12,000 by 2015.*

    *Health spending continues to increase much faster than the overall
economy. Since 1970, healthcare spending has grown at an annual rate of
9.9 percent, or about 2.5 percentage points faster than the U.S. Gross Domestic Product (GDP). In recent decades, the growth rates for health
spending and GDP have slowed, but health spending growth remains consistently above GDP growth, as shown in Figure 2.12.*

    *The increase in personal healthcare expenditures, along with the grow-
ing burden of a growing healthcare sector makes this a major area of concern for an aging baby boom generation. To deal with these increasing
costs, investors are going to have to find ways to generate high levels of income, and that's where double-digit investing the 25% Cash Machine way
can give you the edge.*

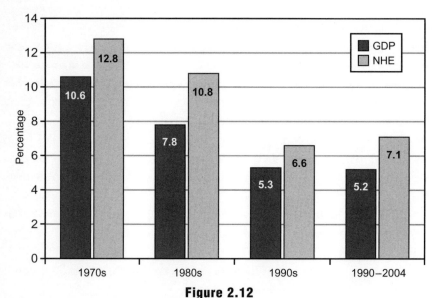

Figure 2.12
Average Annual Growth Rates for Nominal NHE
and GDP for Select Time Periods

Source: Centers for Medicare and Medicaid Services, Office of the Actuary, National Health Statistics Group, at http://www.cms.hhs.gov/NationalHealthExpendData/ (see Historical; NHE sum-
mary including share of GDP, CY 1960–2004: file nhegdp04.zip).

A Taxing Consideration

One of the areas most of us have had to deal with in recent years is the rise in property taxes. In many areas of the country where the real estate markets have been red hot, property taxes have skyrocketed. According to the Minnesota Taxpayers Association, the average tax bill for a median-valued single-family home in the United States was $2,778 in 2004, up 9 percent from $2,549 in 2002. I suspect that when all the facts and figures are tallied for 2005 and 2006, those numbers and their percentage increases will be even higher.

A huge bite out of your discretionary income in the form of a ballooned-up property tax bill can really do some damage to your financial situation. The problem has become so bad that I've heard about many people who have literally been forced to sell their homes and relocate to a less expensive area of the country just to make ends meet. Believe me friends; this is not the kind of adjustment you want to be making, especially if you are in your retirement years.

Although many communities out there are now trying to sue their local governments and calling for the ouster of their local property tax assessors, I think this will likely amount to a futile battle against City Hall. Rather than trying to change the way property taxes are assessed—a task largely out of the control of the average citizen—why not take the steps necessary to deal with these types of unforeseen increases?

The only way to really be sure you can handle unexpected increases in the cost of living is by creating a situation where your money can grow regardless of market conditions. Growth of your principle while simultaneously achieving high-dividend yields each month is what double-digit income investing the 25% Cash Machine way is all about.

3

The Low-Income Environment

I hope by now I've convinced you that we are not in a low-inflation environment. I also hope that any vestige of the low-inflation myth you may have harbored up until this point is gone for good. You should know now how much more we're really paying for the things we all need the most. I don't want to be the bearer of any more bad news, but now that you are aware of the rising costs you face, you have to ask yourselves a simple yet critically important question: How am I going to pay for it all?

If you're an investor relying on traditional income-generating investments to pay for life's necessities—and hopefully a little bit extra—you might be in trouble. Check that; you might be in *big* trouble. Why? Well, because traditional income-generating investments are simply not offering the kinds of returns they have in the past. In fact, the return you get on so many classic financial instruments in many cases is barely keeping up with inflation.

There are still some traditional income-generating investments that pay a little more than overall inflation, but after Uncle Sam takes his bite out of the pie you're left with barely enough to keep your head above water. You almost certainly won't have much left over to actually grow your money, and that won't leave you in a position to increase your wealth over time.

In the past several years, we've been mired in what I call a "low-income environment." A low-income environment simply means that the return you're getting on those traditional income-generating investments is well below what it has been historically. It also means that the return on your money is low when compared with inflation as measured by either the overall CPI number, or especially as measured by what we know to be the true cost of living.

Now let's take a look under the hood of the most common traditional instruments that investors rely on to generate the income they need to fund their lives. I think you'll soon agree with me when I characterize our current climate as a low-income environment.

Money Market Funds—You're Safe, but Poor

Money market funds; just the thought of them conjures up images of safe, steady returns. A mini-cash machine, if you will. Unfortunately, the rate of return you get from money market funds these days looks more like a coin return slot than a cash machine.

There's no doubt about it, the interest paid on money market accounts is safe. Short of a complete collapse of the U.S. banking system, your investment in a money market account will be there when you need it. The trouble with money market funds is that despite the rising tide of interest rates that began in 2004, these investments are still only offering a very modest return.

The national average for money market rates midway through 2006 was just over 3 percent. Think about that for a moment in the context of what we already know about how much things really cost? It's not hard to figure out that unless you have a huge mountain of cash lying around, a 3 percent return on your money just isn't going get it done. In fact, a 3 percent return doesn't even keep pace with the overall CPI inflation number, let alone the real cost of things today.

Investing in a money market fund is not what I consider a step toward a positive cash-generating machine. In fact, given the market conditions present so far in the twenty-first century, I'd say a money market investment functions more like a financial black hole that sucks up all the fiscal material around it until there's nothing left for you to live on. It's a case of simple math. If the overall CPI number is running near 4 percent, and the national average for money market rates is just over 3 percent, what do you think is going to happen to your money? That's right, it's going to evaporate before you know it.

In Figure 3.1 we see the trend in money market returns from mid-2003 to mid-2006. This chart clearly depicts the uptrend in money market returns since midway through 2004. Since then, money market rates have climbed steadily. The reason why this happened is due to the Federal Reserve.

The central bank, led by Alan Greenspan until early 2006, began tightening the purse strings in June 2004. At that time, money market

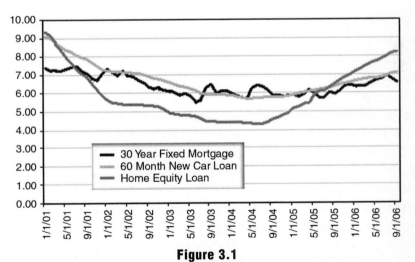

Figure 3.1
Money Market Rates, National Average 3 Years

Source: Datatrac.

rates were just scantly above 1 percent, as was the federal funds rate, which is the rate that the Federal Reserve charges its member banks on overnight loans.

Sensing that inflation was beginning to rise after several years of easy money and credit policies engineered by the very same Federal Reserve, Mr. Greenspan and company decided it was time to start increasing the cost of capital. That's when banks started increasing the interest paid on money market accounts. But despite over two years of constant interest rate hikes, money market accounts are still paying just over 3 percent.

Okay, you say that money markets are not your main vehicle for generating income. True, but they are perhaps the safest way to generate income, and many people fearful of losing money in the equity markets still rely on money market accounts for at least some of their total return. If you are one of those settling for what the bank gives you, you do so at your own peril. Inflation and taxes will team up to blight that "safe" money market payout, and you'll be left worse off than when you started.

Certificates of Deposit—A Commitment to Mediocrity

Another traditional income asset is the Certificate of Deposit, or CD. I'm quite sure many of you either currently own, or have owned a CD in the past, as they are a very common way to make a guaranteed return on your money. The downside to owning a CD is that depending on the maturity of the CD you choose, your money will be off limits to you for the specified duration of that particular instrument.

The most common CDs require you to tie up your money for three months, six months, one year, or five years. In exchange, CDs pay you a predetermined fixed rate of return. Like money market funds, the rate of return on CDs over the past several years has climbed considerably, as shown in Figure 3.2. But despite an upward trend in the interest that CDs pay, the best of them is still only going to pay about 5 percent.

In my opinion, 5 percent or just slightly above that is about as good as it is going to get on the CD front. Why do I say that? Well, because the Federal Reserve has, by all accounts, just about finished tightening those

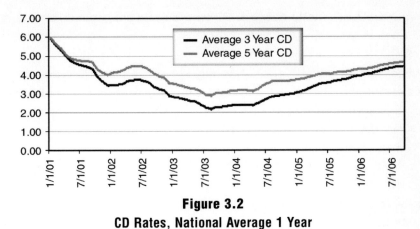

Figure 3.2
CD Rates, National Average 1 Year

Source: Datatrac.

purse strings. The thinking is that the central bank will stop somewhere between 5 percent and 6 percent on the federal funds rate. CD rates won't climb too much over that mark, which means that you're only going to get a mediocre 5 to 6 percent return on your money from CDs.

If 5 to 6 percent is okay with you, or if you have the kind of principal that allows you to generate enough income to live like a king on that kind of modest return on your assets, then fine. In fact, I would encourage you to buy CDs. Unfortunately, most of us aren't in a position to settle for just mediocre returns. Most of us have to do something to stay ahead of the rising cost of everything, and most of us need to position our assets so that our principal has the chance to keep growing.

Bonds—Are They the Answer?

For so many years, bonds of all varieties have been the staple of the income investor's diet. U.S. government–issued debt instruments like 30-year Treasury bonds, 10-year Treasury notes, 2-year Treasury notes, and Treasury bills have all taken prominent positions on many a portfolio mantelpiece. In addition to government issued bonds, income-seeking investors have also been extremely fond of high-quality corporate bonds.

Hey, what's not to like about Treasury bonds? They pay a steady rate of return and they are backed by the U.S. government. In the case of corporate bonds, these debt securities are backed by some of the highest quality companies in the world today.

Well, there is nothing inherently wrong with bonds, either the government or corporate variety. The only problem I have with these types of bonds—and of course it's a huge problem—is the rate of return you get on your money.

Over the past several years, T-bills, notes, and bonds have all given investors rather anemic returns. In fact, the returns you get on these instruments are not much better than money markets or CDs. Figure 3.3 clearly demonstrates that although yields have risen sharply in recent years, they've just about topped out right around the 5 percent range.

Midway through 2006, six-month Treasury bills were still paying only 5 percent. The 2-year Treasury note finally broke the 5 percent barrier right about this time as well. It's a similar situation in both the 10-year and the 30-year Treasury instruments. I think 5 percent is right about what you can expect now that the Fed has basically completed its multiyear interest rate hiking cycle.

Think corporate bonds are much better? Well, some are, but most are just not offering that attractive a return on your money. If you look at the interest rates being paid on Moody's AAA-rated bonds, the average rate midway through 2006 was about 5.9 percent. Not exactly

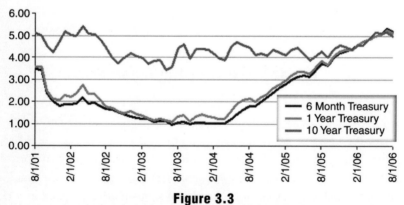

Figure 3.3
Treasury Yields on Bills, Notes, and Bonds

Source: U.S. Treasury.

a world-beating rate of return, and definitely not enough to fund most of our retirement goals.

In the current low-income environment, money market funds, CDs, government and corporate bonds just aren't getting the job done. Now this has not always been the case. There have been many years in past decades where these traditional income-generating instruments have provided us with double-digit yields.

At the beginning of the 1980s, six-month CDs were paying between 12 percent and 15 percent. Now that is what I call easy money. If conditions ever got back to what they were in the early 1980s you wouldn't need to read a book like this, and I wouldn't need to write a book like this. Hey, we all yearn for those days of easy money, but unfortunately, they are probably gone for good.

Bond's also enjoyed a more glamorous past life, having provided investors with double-digit returns in the 1980s as well. Hey, bonds weren't a bad place to be in the 1990s either, with the safest of all bonds—the 30-year Treasury—yielding almost 9 percent as the decade began. It's basically been all downhill for bonds ever since then, and that is a trend that I am afraid will continue for quite some time.

What about Motgage-Backed Securities?

You might be asking yourself if mortgage-backed securities provide any better way of getting a decent yield than money markets, CDs, or bonds. The mortgage-backed security market includes Ginnie Mae, Fannie Mae, and Freddie Mac asset-backed instruments. These securities do pay a little bit more than Treasuries and CDs, but here's the rub: Even if you buy these securities at the top of the interest rate cycle, you could still be in trouble.

You have to understand that mortgage-backed securities aren't bonds. They are pools of mortgage debt. Anyone who has ever owned these mortgage-backed securities knows that when interest rates drop, the underlying mortgages all get refinanced at the lower rate. The issuers (the federal mortgage agencies) then return capital back to investors, meaning we have to reinvest that capital at a lower prevailing rate. Wow, thanks for nothing.

Assuming you've called the market right at the top of the interest rate cycle, you should see a rally in bonds ensue when rates begin to fall. But if you think you are going to benefit from the rising price of bonds through mortgage-backed securities you are mistaken, because all you are going to be getting is chunks of your original principal handed back to you when the refinancing process begins. To compound the problem, with mortgage-backed securities you won't enjoy the capital appreciation that occurs in the Treasury and corporate bond markets, and all you'll be left with in the end is yet another sub-par rate of return.

Tying It All Together

The 5 to 6 percent returns promised by traditional income-generating instruments constitute what I call the low-income environment. I am afraid that this reality is something we've got to deal with for the foreseeable future. Sure, circumstances may change, interest rates may spike and money market accounts could become your best bet on Wall Street. Is this likely? No. Is it probable? No. Are the chances remote? Yes. In my opinion, they are very remote.

Let's take a quick look at what relying on a 5 percent annual dividend yield would look like in real dollar amounts. Let's say you had a nest egg of $500,000. Now this isn't a huge amount of money, but it isn't tiny either. In fact, it far exceeds what the average American saves in a lifetime. Assume that this is the money you are going to rely on to generate the income you need to pay for all of your living expenses each year. Well, some simple math tells us that at 5 percent rate of return on this money will give us $25,000 a year. I think that most of us would say that $25,000 isn't really going to get the job done when it comes to paying for life's necessities.

Now let's assume we can achieve a rate of return that is twice that. A double-digit, 10 percent annual rate of return on $500,000 is $50,000 per year. That will get you a lot closer to an annual income stream that can actually help you pay for the things you both need and want. Now think about getting that $50,000 per year income, and growing that $500,000 by 15 percent in a year. That will leave you with a $575,000 nest egg with which you can generate even more income the following year, specifically, $57,500. Sound like a good deal? Well, it most definitely is, and it is what the 25% Cash Machine is all about.

Some of you reading this now are no doubt familiar with what investment professionals call the "Rule of 72." How it works is you take the projected return on your money and divide it into the number 72. That gives you the time in which it takes to double your money. At a 6 percent rate of return, your money doubles in 12 years (provided of course you don't touch it). At a 10 percent rate of return, your money doubles in only 7.2 years. And what if you were to achieve a rate of say, 25 percent per year? Well, it would only take you 2.88 years to double your nest egg.

Of course, I realize that in the real world, doubling your money in less than three years this isn't a very likely scenario, especially considering that the income you generate will largely go to paying for the rising cost of living that we illustrated in Chapter 2. But the point here is that just settling for the 5 to 6 percent income stream traditional dividend-yielding investments deliver—an income stream with virtually no ability to grow your assets—is just not going to get it done in this inflationary environment.

To get more out of our money, we have to turn our attention to other investment vehicles. We have to go "off the reservation" as the saying goes. But before we go way off the reservation there is one more well-known traditional asset class that many people feel can still do the job for them.

I am talking here about those old-guard dividend-oriented stocks. You know about them already. These are the big, safe, secure, and always strong blue-chip companies that give you a taste of their profits each quarter. As we are about to find out, those old-guard dividend paying stocks aren't always safe, secure, and strong. In fact, the reality in many cases is just about 180 degrees different.

4

Dead-End Dividend Stocks

Now that you know the pitfalls of owning traditional income-generating securities such as money markets, CDs, and bonds in a low-income environment—an environment made all the more dangerous given the rising cost of the things we actually need—you might be asking yourself if the stock market is a viable way to get the kind of income you need. Well, the answer is yes, it can be, but not in the way most people think.

I'd wager that many of you have heard the term "widows and orphans" in the context of the stock market. This is a term used to describe certain kinds of traditional dividend-paying stocks. These stocks got their name because they were thought to be the strong, stable securities suitable for widows who couldn't afford to miss their dividends because of the loss of their husband's income, and orphans, who relied on the dividend income generated by these stocks to pay for the cost of their upbringing.

At one time, and even still today, many people considered widow-and-orphan stocks to be an essential component in a well-rounded income portfolio. The stocks we are talking about here are the old-guard, dividend-oriented stocks such as utility companies and other massive blue-chip firms that were thought to be immune from damage even in a declining stock market. Sure, the share price might be stagnant for a while, but you were still going to get that monthly dividend check.

So, what's wrong with owning some of these widow-and-orphan stocks? Well, nothing, except that what was once true of these companies is no longer true. Over the past decade, the appeal of traditional dividend-paying equities has faded, and in my opinion, for very good reasons. The reality is that these old-guard dividend-paying stocks just haven't kept up with their reputation as safe, stable companies that pay an attractive dividend. In fact, in recent years, the exact opposite has been the case for many traditional dividend-paying stalwarts.

An Ignominious List

We'd all like to think there are at least some things in life we can count on, especially when it comes to our money. I mean, surely the biggest, strongest, most prominent American corporate entities still pay great dividends to their shareholders, right? Boy, do I wish that were true. In fact, if it were true, my job of generating income and growth for my clients, as well as subscribers to my 25% Cash Machine service, would be quite a bit easier.

Unfortunately, the reality is that we cannot count anything as sacred when it comes to our money. Times change, market conditions change, companies and industries change, and Wall Street changes. In order to keep up with this change, we have to be flexible, and we have to be able to recognize when the tides have shifted on a particular way of doing things. Such is the case with the so-called widow-and-orphan stocks.

Just look at some of the names in Table 4.1. These aren't exactly mom-and-pop operations are they? Rather, they read like a who's who of American corporate power and strength. This list includes some of the companies that built up our country's economy for decades, helping making it the most prosperous nation the world has ever seen.

Table 4.1
15 Dead-End Dividend Stocks—Data as of July, 2006

Company	5-Year Price Range ($)	5-Year Stock Performance (% Loss)	Current Dividend Yield (%)
AT&T (T)	50–20	60	4.77
Pfizer (PFE)	47–26	44	4.05
Bristol Meyers (BMY)	70–25	64	4.44
General Electric (GE)	60–34	43	3.00
Ford (F)	30–10	66	6.05
Merck (MRK)	90–29	67	4.14
International Business Machines (IBM)	130–80	38	1.51
Marsh & McLennan (MMC)	67–30	55	2.57
General Motors (GM)	75–32	57	3.4
Coca Cola (KO)	63–44	30	2.88
Fannie Mae (FNM)	90–49	45	2.12
American International (AIG)	105–61	42	1.11
SBC Communications (SBC)	60–24	60	4.77
Verizon (VZ)	57–33	42	4.87
JP Morgan (JPM)	56–35	37	3.21

Source: DTNIQ.

One of the biggest, most widely held stocks on this list is General Electric. The diversified industrial and media giant was once thought to be a no-brainer pick for just about any solid dividend stock portfolio. Hey, it still is considered that way by most brokerage firms. In fact, I challenge you to call your broker right now and ask him or her if GE shares are a good long-term investment. I'll bet you a cup of Starbucks coffee that the answer will be a great big unequivocal yes. Well, since about 2000, GE certainly hasn't been my idea of a good investment at all (see Figure 4.1).

In fact, one look at the price chart of this so-called stalwart and you can see why I wouldn't put my clients in it—unless my goal was to manage their portfolios into the ground. But hey, you might be thinking that despite GE's less-than-stellar price performance, you can still get a solid dividend, right? Well, if you call a dividend of just over 3 percent solid, then

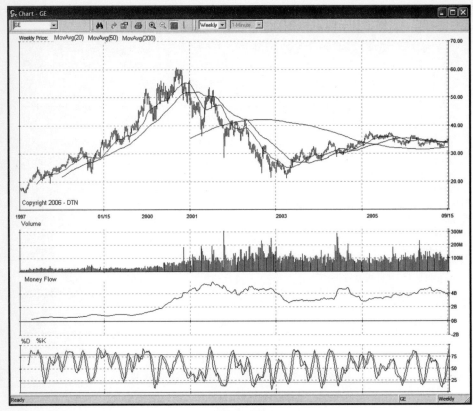

Figure 4.1
GE Weekly

Source: DTNIQ.

you really need this book. In my world, a 3 percent dividend and a share price that is down about 20 percent over five years isn't very solid. In fact, it's more like quicksand.

I wish I could say that GE was an isolated case, but unfortunately for so many investors who put their money in these dead-end dividend stocks, GE is just one of a large group of once-mighty juggernauts that have now fallen on hard times. AT&T, Ford Motor, IBM, Coca-Cola, JP Morgan, and many more have all given up huge chunks of their value since 2000. Not only that, these stocks are paying what in my opinion is a rather anemic dividend.

To put the issue in stronger terms, what we really have here is a list of 15 big losers, *10 of which are current components of the Dow Jones Industrial Average*. Not exactly comforting is it? Even less comforting is the fact that just about 10 years ago, the portfolio in Table 4.1 was the absolute rage on Wall Street. These stocks were what I call institutional Barbie dolls, as just about every big fund manager out there bought them for their income-oriented clientele. But as a quick view of each of these stocks shows, owning this portfolio today is like dragging around a bag of rocks. It's dead money, pure and simple.

One thing critical to note here is that many investors fall into the trap of thinking that because their stocks are paying a 2 to 5 percent dividend, that somehow this is going to protect the underlying share price from falling. As our examples clearly show, nothing could be farther from the truth. I bring this up here because it's a common story heard time and time again with income and growth investors who cling to former Wall Street darlings. I don't know why this mindset is so prevalent, but I do have a few clues as to why these stocks continue to be so popular even in the face of such heavy declines.

Brokerage Firm Complacence

Wall Street would like us to believe that a 4 percent dividend on a stock is a good yield on our money. After all, this yield does compete favorably with money markets, CDs, and bonds in our current low-income environment. In fact, we've been in such a low-income environment for so long now, that dividend stocks offering even the promise of a little capital appreciation along with a modest dividend yield become attractive instruments.

As we've already seen, however, many of the biggest blue-chip stocks currently paying 4 percent are also big-time losers. So why do investors keep purchasing these dead-end dividend stocks? Is there some flaw in our ability to reason when it comes to the market? I don't think so. In fact, I think when presented with facts and sound logic, most investors will make the wise decision with their money.

Having worked for some of the biggest brokerage firms in the business, I can tell you that as a rule (of course, there are exceptions) brokers in general are very complacent when it comes to hunting for great financial instruments that pay big yields and have strong upside potential. In a way, I can't really blame the broker, because he or she isn't generally compensated for crafting a winning strategy for the clients. They are compensated, indeed instructed, to sell clients the mutual funds and securities that their management and investment banking teams want them to sell. The result is that you hear about the stocks, bonds, and funds your broker gets paid to sell you. Often, brokers are paid to push you dead-end dividend stocks.

The other reason why I think people continue buying dead-end dividend stocks is because the stories are just very easy to understand. Think about it, what's easier to talk about—new hybrid dividend securities or drug-giant Pfizer? There's no doubt about it, everyone knows about Pfizer. In fact, many income investors have a bevy of Pfizer's products perched in their medicine cabinets right now.

So is it any wonder why today Pfizer is one of the most widely held stocks in America? Pfizer is a story that is easy to understand, and easy to sell to a less-than-savvy investing public. The big brokerage firms on Wall Street will call you up and try to tell you the stock is a safe haven, absolutely suitable for widows and orphans (although they probably won't use that specific term). Their advice is always to just buy the stock, collect your dividend, and forget about it. But as we've already seen, that approach is just not commensurate with a successful income-investing strategy.

I don't know about you, but a 3 to 4 percent yield on my income and growth money just doesn't cut it. And couple that with the Pfizer shares losing nearly half their value over the first five years of the decade (see Figure 4.2), and you have a prescription for poor financial health. What a broker won't tell you is that the Pfizer story topped out in 1999 when the new bull market in generic drugs took off. The next time you get a call from a broker about Pfizer, or the next time you talk to one of your friends that owns the stock, ask them why the shares have sunk so much in recent years. Chances are they won't know anything about the generic drug boom.

Figure 4.2
PFE Weekly

Source: DTNIQ.

The Dead-End Dividend Poster Child

Pfizer is one of my favorite examples of a dead-end dividend stock, no question about it. But perhaps the best poster child for the dead-end dividend stock is automaker General Motors.

For years and years, GM was one of those stocks that deserved a place in just about any dividend-stock portfolio. The company sold millions of automobiles around the world, and for decades it ruled the automotive market. The share price was basically stable for decades, and the company always paid its shareholders a very attractive yield.

In fact, up until February 2006, GM shares paid investors an 8 percent dividend yield—not too bad at all for a massive blue-chip company whose share price had tumbled since the beginning of the decade. But alas, this relatively high dividend could not be kept up given the poor financial condition of the company, and that's when GM decided to slash its dividend in half.

That's right, with a stroke of the pen GM cut its dividend payments to shareholders by 50 percent. That meant that an investor who received $3000 of dividend income from the company each quarter would now get a check for about $1500. Depending on how many shares of GM you happened to have in your income portfolio, that 50 percent haircut could be the difference between meeting your monthly expenses and falling woefully short.

The GM case clearly demonstrates how a once-mighty widow-and-orphan stalwart can, in a matter of just a few short years, become a stock to be avoided at all costs, as shown in Figure 4.3. Like I said before, we'd all like to think there are things we can count on out there when it comes to our money. Unfortunately, the GM case illustrates the peril of believing that just because a blue-chip company has paid a nice dividend in the past, that it will forever continue paying that dividend. Hey, things just don't work that way, and the sooner you disabuse yourself of this notion, the quicker you can start taking the necessary steps to begin building your 25% Cash Machine.

Even the Winners Are Losers

Right about now you might be saying to yourself, what about those dividend-paying stocks that have climbed in value in recent years and that do pay a healthy dividend? Don't they have a place in a thriving income portfolio? That's a great question, and one that I am confronted with frequently whenever I explain my philosophy of double-digit income investing. The short answer is no, they don't. Let me explain why.

Maybe the best way to address this question is to actually take a look at a huge, stalwart dividend-paying stock that's been burning up the charts in terms of its price appreciation for a number of years now, and that is oil giant Exxon Mobil. This company has consistently moved the

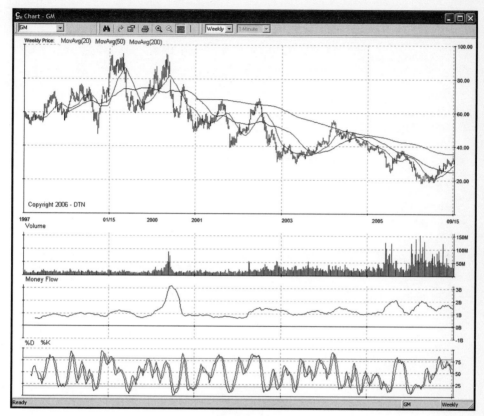

Figure 4.3
GM Weekly

Source: DTNIQ.

bar higher in terms of record corporate profits. In fact, Exxon Mobil's fourth-quarter 2005 profit of $10.71 billion was the most money any company has ever earned in history (see Figure 4.4).

Considering their record profits, it's no surprise that the share price has seen a substantial increase. In fact, Exxon Mobil shares climbed nearly 50 percent from 2001 to 2006. That is a huge increase, and definitely worth owning on its own merits in your growth stock portfolio, but what of its income-producing potential?

Over this same time period, with its stock price soaring and profits coming in at unprecedented rates, the dividend yield on Exxon Mobil

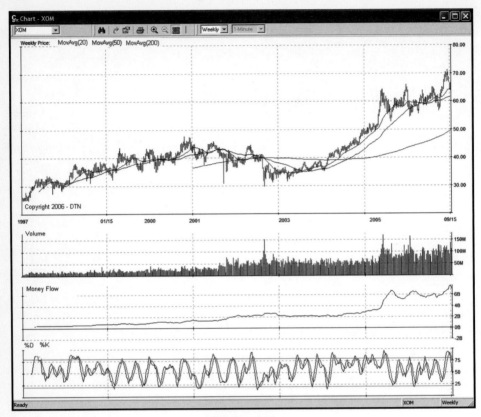

Figure 4.4
XOM Weekly

Source: DTNIQ.

was on average just slightly more than 2 percent. That's right, a company that's pulling in gargantuan revenues and mammoth profits the likes of which the world has never before seen is paying its shareholders only a 2 percent dividend yield. That's not a very good deal in my book. In fact, it downright stinks.

So my question to you is this: If a company that's making record profits, sitting on a boatload of cash, and whose share price has appreciated nearly 50 percent over five years is still not able to pay out dividends of just slightly north of 2 percent, what does this say for the prospects of relying on dividend stocks as a means of generating income in your portfolio? I say it doesn't portend well at all. And given the fact that even this winner can be considered a loser, the time has come to start looking at your dividend portfolio with a fresh set of eyes.

A New Way of Thinking

The reliance on traditional dividend stocks is a relic of a bygone era. We can no longer buy and hold blue-chip names, collect our dividends, and live happily ever after in retirement. Like so many things in our world, the invisible hand that moves markets also requires that we constantly reevaluate the axioms that we grew up thinking were immutable.

Never has there been a clearer case of needing to rethink the paradigm than in the field of income investing. The safe income instruments we've relied on in the past just aren't providing us the kinds of returns we require. The real cost of living is climbing, chewing up those scant returns and providing us little in the way of cushion to fund our future.

Finally, as we've just shown you, the traditional dividend-paying stocks we've come to rely on have let us down. In fact, they've been downright disappointing for so many years now that we just have to realize that they are probably not going to be a major part of the solution to the problems confronting income investors, at least not unless market conditions change dramatically.

Fortunately, there is a solution to the prevailing problems weighing on income investors. But that solution requires a whole new way of approaching things. It requires looking beyond traditional methods of income generation in favor of the new and exciting bevy of income securities out there that offer high-yields—often with a much greater degree of safety than traditional widow-and-orphan stocks.

In Chapter 5, you'll see that the way we approach income investing in the 25% Cash Machine doesn't resemble the so-called tried-and-true methods that Wall Street constantly tells you is the answer. You will see that when it comes to income investing, it's a brave new world out there.

PART TWO

THE SOLUTION: DOUBLE-DIGIT INCOME INVESTING

5

Income Investing for the Twenty-First Century

I've spent the first few chapters of this book slaughtering many of the sacred cows Wall Street tries to herd your way when it comes time to generating income after a lifetime of asset building. By now it should be clear that the concept that we are in a low-inflation environment is indeed a myth. You should also now be fully aware of the dreadful failure traditional assets like money markets, CDs, and Treasury bonds have been in this low-income environment. Finally, you should be well versed in the ineffectiveness of relying on old-guard dividend stocks for both income and growth. These stocks just aren't what they used to be, and the world is not likely to go back to the way it was just because you've reached age 65. But hey, just telling you what's wrong with doing it the old-fashioned way won't help you understand how to do it any differently.

Sure, by now you may be questioning some of the premises you thought were based in truth regarding the various income-generating instruments we've covered. You probably also now realize that unless you are sitting on a super-sized pile of dough, your retirement cake isn't going to feed you enough income to pay for the things you need most, and it certainly won't permit you to attain the luxuries in life that we all feel we have coming our way after decades in the workforce. And heaven forbid you ever have to deal with a major medical expense such as long-term nursing care for an aging parent, spouse, or sibling. Then you'll really be in need of some help, and unfortunately by then, it might just be too late.

So what's the answer? How can you go about generating enough monthly income to keep yourself living the way you want? How will you ever be able to keep that nest egg growing so that you'll never be in danger of outliving your money?

The answer is by employing the principles of double-digit income investing. Armed with the knowledge you garner from the remainder of this book, you will absolutely be able to start building your very own 25% Cash Machine.

What the 25% Cash Machine Is Not

Before we get into what double-digit income investing is, and what the major components of the 25% Cash Machine actually are, I want to dispel a few preconceptions that I suspect many of the more experienced investors out there might initially think apply to what I do.

When I started in the brokerage business with Smith Barney back in 1984, junk bonds and Michael Milken were just becoming all the rage in the high-yield market. Actually at that time, for the most part, high-yield bonds were basically the entire high-yield market. Of course these high-yield bonds, also known by their more derogatory term "junk bonds," brought with them massive amounts of risk.

Along with the inherent risk of investing in low-rated corporate debt issues that were often used to finance leveraged buyout deals, a lot of chicanery and foul play came flooding into the high-yield market. Well, we all know what happened to Mr. Milken and the firm Drexel Burnham Lambert after it became entangled in an insider trading scandal. That scandal tarnished the reputation of the high-yield debt securities market for some time, and it put the kibosh on junk bonds for many income investors who rightly perceived this market as just too risky for their retirement dollars.

Even though today the high-yield corporate bond market continues to thrive with institutional bond traders, these debt instruments are not an asset class we employ in the 25% Cash Machine. With low-rated corporate debt always in danger of default, these bonds are just too risky, and they constitute way too much of a gamble with your critical nest egg funds. So if you harbored any thoughts that double-digit income investing means playing the junk bond game, you can put your mind at ease right now. Junk bonds are not, and will never be, an asset class we use to achieve our objective of double-digit income returns.

Another strategy that is not employed in any significant fashion in the 25% Cash Machine is what's known as writing covered calls. This is an options strategy designed to generate cash on a basket of assets that an investor already owns. Some income-oriented investment managers tout covered calls as a great way to pump up an investor's monthly income. I disagree.

Basically, writing covered calls works like this. You the investor sell "call" options on the stocks you own (the right to buy a security at a specified price and time period) and collect the premium that those options generate. The premiums you collect from selling these call options is considered income according to this strategy. Sounds okay so far, but what happens when those call options get exercised? That's right; you have to sell the underlying security that you originally wrote the call on.

If you have a stock in your portfolio that you don't mind selling for that predetermined price, the strategy works just fine. However, as you will soon see, with double-digit income investing we don't want the decision on when to sell a particular security determined by someone calling in the options. Also, this strategy works best if you aren't expecting a lot of upside (or downside) in the security you own. We like to position our assets in securities that have a lot of upside potential, and we don't want to have to give those securities up just because we collected a little premium on them. The bottom line is that there are just a whole lot better and less risky ways to get double-digit returns than by writing covered calls.

Finally, double-digit income investing is not some kind of hypersophisticated, indecipherable, hedge-fund style mathematical system that shorts exotic currencies and straddles commodity contracts in some obscure market tucked away in a remote region of the globe. All the concepts you will learn about building your 25% Cash Machine are easy to understand and easy to employ as long as you apply yourself to understanding them. And all of the tools we use to achieve these double-digit returns can be found on the major U.S. equity market exchanges such as the New York Stock Exchange, NASDAQ, and American Stock Exchange.

What the 25% Cash Machine Is

Now we've arrived at the juicy point of our story. In Chapter 1 we told you that today, income investors have opportunities open to them in virtually every sector of the market. Indeed, the broad issuance of new income securities over the past decade has allowed income investors to have their cake (double-digit income) and eat it, too (capital appreciation).

These two objectives: Double-digit income on the order of 10 percent per year, plus capital appreciation on the order of 15 percent per year, equals a total annual return goal of 25 percent! That's in essence what this machine we're building is all about. The first objective is to find the securities that can generate those double-digit yields we all need to fund our retirement years. But the 25% Cash Machine doesn't just stop there. The securities we choose must also posses the potential to grow by 15 percent or more per year.

A tall order you ask? Well, 10 years ago I would have said an impossible order. But now, thanks to the wide array of new income-oriented tools—and a battle-tested strategy that teaches you how to find the right securities and what you do once you find them—I can say without equivocation that the goals of the 25% Cash Machine are definitely attainable.

I know from the personal experience of managing this kind of money for many years now that this system works, and it works better than any other method I've ever encountered. Now let's dig a little deeper into some of the characteristics of the 25% Cash Machine.

First off, the 25% Cash Machine approaches the market with an eye toward finding strong companies in strong market sectors. We don't want to buy just any old dividend-paying stock just because it has a better-than-average yield. We are looking for superstar securities that throw off at least 10 percent annual yields while their underlying share price heads higher. Double-digit income investing isn't content with owning the likes of a Pfizer, GM, or any of the other dead-end dividend stocks we looked at in Chapter 4. These stocks are antithetical to the goals of the 25% Cash Machine, and they just don't meet our criteria for inclusion.

Another characteristic of double-digit investing is to look for securities with what I call "yield power." These are securities that are currently in thriving businesses, that is to say, they are in profitable ventures that make a lot of money. These securities pay out between 50 percent and 95 percent of their cash flow to you, the investor, in the form of dividends, interest or distributions. Determining yield power involves a basic calculation called a *payout ratio*. This is the percentage of every dollar of cash flow that gets paid out to shareholders.

Here's an easy example that will help illustrate what I mean. If a company has $2.00 of net income per share, and it pays out $1.50 of that $2.00, then we would say that it has a 75 percent payout ratio ($1.50 divided by $2.00 = 0.75). This 75 percent payout ratio figure is a good one, because it tells you that a company (or other type of security) is probably reinvesting some money into expanding operations and growing its business. And that growth and expansion helps us to identify the securities that, in addition to paying out double-digit returns, also have the best chance to appreciate by 15 percent annually.

The real characteristic of the 25% Cash Machine that makes it so powerful is that we aren't afraid to embrace the many new income-oriented equity tools that have hit the market over the past 10 years. These new tools have made it possible for the average investor to get the double-digit returns on his or her money that until just a few years ago were open to only the super rich.

This new development in the financial industry is what I call the "public-ization" of the private equity markets. Now for decades, private equity markets were the strictly the province of the blue-blood rich investors who commuted between Manhattan penthouses and Malibu beach houses. These guys had access to the private equity pools that were expertly managed by some of the smartest guys on Wall Street.

These private equity pools beat the pants off the returns that you could get in S&P 500 stocks, but to have access to these managers you had to pony up over $1 million just to say hello. But now there are new tools open to the public that invest in the same fashion as some of these private equity firms do. These securities pay whopping dividends, and they've got plenty of capital appreciation to go along with it. Finally, we all have the opportunity to invest like the super wealthy.

Many of the tools I am about to acquaint you with are new to the marketplace and have only been available to investors for a few years. Some of these tools have actually been around for quite a while, but have just not been widely adopted by income investors. I suspect the chief reason for this neglect is that many people just don't understand even the basics about how some of these asset classes work.

If you are one of the many investors who've settled for low, single-digit returns on your money just because you fear the unknown, I say don't let that fear control your lives. Remember that famous line from FDR's 1933 inaugural address: "The only thing we have to fear is fear itself"? Well, that line also applies to double-digit income investing. The only caveat I would add is that if you do let your fear of the unknown rule your investment decisions, the tiny return you'll have to settle for will put you in real jeopardy of outliving your money. Then the fear of not having enough money to survive becomes very, very real.

It's time now to shed that fear of the unknown by lifting the veil on some of the best asset classes available for generating double-digit yields while pursuing growth in your income portfolio. These are the income investing characters that occupy center stage in the 25% Cash Machine, and after you finish this chapter, I suspect these characters will begin playing a prominent role in your own income investment production.

There are many other new tools besides just these private equity funds that have come to the market over the past decade, and we will explore some of the best in much greater detail in later chapters. But first let me whet your appetite with a quick look at some of new tools we'll use to build our double-digit income, 25% Cash Machine:

- *Canadian Royalty Trusts:* One of my favorite high-income investments, these securities have been in the sweet spot of the energy boom that began midway through this decade and that shows no signs of cooling off. Add to the mix a favorable tax treatment and you have a new breed of income security better than any old-guard dividend stock.
- *Canadian Business Trusts:* You may see the obvious trend here with Canadian companies positioning themselves as "income trusts." That's why I like this sector as well. Canadian Business Trusts are in businesses like cold storage, air cargo, public utility operations, timber, food distribution, and recycled energy.
- *Business Development Companies:* These are specially regulated retail investment companies that typically make private equity-style investments in small to middle-market companies.
- *Closed-end funds:* These funds pool investors' money and then invest in high yielding bonds and other high yield instruments not available to individuals.
- *Convertible securities:* Seldom used by individual investors, you can capture the same outsized yields that big institutional investors get with less risk and exposure.
- *Equity Income Hybrid Securities or Income Deposit Securities:* They don't fit the mold of most conventional high-income vehicles, yet they are truly some of the best performing equities with generous yields. It's a way for a solid, profitable company with a not-so-sexy business to attract investors through the structuring of its stock to it pays out extraordinary dividend yields.
- *Real Estate Investment Trusts (REITs):* Most REITs are invested in brick-and-mortar assets. The income investor gets to directly invest in a diversified pool of real estate, either through properties or

mortgages. REITs trade like regular common stocks and provide excellent liquidity, unlike most forms of traditional real estate.

- *Shipping and tankers:* I love this sector with its high yields and steady business flow, but these stocks can sometimes get a little wild on the up and down scale.
- *Master Limited Partnerships (MLPs):* These babies are only taxed once at the corporate level, leaving plenty of cash to pay back in the form of dividends to its shareholders.

These sound good, don't they (and I've barely just scratched the surface). Well, they are good, and they are all components of the 25% Cash Machine. By putting these kinds of tools in our shed, and with the proper strategy to know how to operate these tools, you will never have to settle for the 4 to 5 percent yield you'll get from conventional income assets again.

The marketplace created these asset classes in response to investor demand for better ways to generate income. Believe me; Wall Street won't create a new class of security unless it can sell it to the investing public. Income investors know that they have to do a better job of making their money work for them than conventional asset classes can offer, and hence, Wall Street created this new breed of income investments.

Hey, this is definitely not your father's income investing now is it? And because a lot of this stuff is new to so many investors, it is incumbent on each of us to find out more about how these new financial instruments actually work. In the next chapter, that is exactly what we are going to do.

6

Manna from Canada

When it comes to knowing how to structure a double-digit income security, all you have to do is look to our neighbor to the north. That's right; Canada has been the font for much of the manna in the smart investor's high-yield portfolio in recent years. Why? Well, partly because of the structure of its royalty and business trusts, and partly because of the secular bull market in energy. Let's take a closer look at two of these Canada-based asset classes—Canadian Royalty Trusts (CanRoys), and Canadian Business Trusts (CBTs), and see what makes them tick.

Canadian Royalty Trusts

A really terrific development in the past 10 years has been the issuance of several natural resource-based trusts that are traded as highly liquid public securities. Simply put, an income trust is an investment syndicate that pools its money to buy a cash flow generating asset with the cash flow after expenses distributed back to the unitholders.

These unique securities are based on oil trusts that replenish themselves with growing reserves so they can grow the business and pay out rising dividends on a perpetual basis. They grow reserves by reinvesting some of their cash flow into future exploration and also through acquisitions of other reserves and operating companies.

Canadian Royalty Trusts are essentially oil and gas companies that, because of their special tax status, pay out a large percentage of their cash flow to shareholders (unitholders) in the form of monthly distributions. These trusts are structured to control operating companies that go out and purchase oil and gas properties using the trust's capital. The trust then receives royalty payments from the operating company.

Since "pumping volumes" from the properties the trusts own are relatively constant, the royalties collected on existing resources vary mostly with changes in oil and gas prices. That said, if prices continue to move up, so will the royalties and thus the dividend payouts. Conversely, if prices fall, we can fully expect our dividend payout to also fall.

CanRoys trade just as stocks do, but unlike stocks these securities distribute almost everything they earn to unitholders. Although they are not real companies with management teams and daily operations, they are freely and actively traded by fund managers for their super-attractive dividends. The higher dividend yields from Canadian oil trusts that flow from the ongoing operations of the underlying assets is a good sign that business is healthy.

Perpetual Asset Growth Model

Canadian Royalty Trusts differ from U.S. based royalty trusts. The perpetual growth component is unique to CanRoys. In contrast, U.S.-based oil trusts are structured by law as a finite set of assets in the ground. They cannot acquire new properties, as Canadian trusts can, and thus one day become worthless when the oil and gas reserves are fully depleted.

The U.S.-based trusts pay out the cash flow generated from their existing properties, but they do not acquire new properties. Consequently, their cash flows decline over time as their underlying assets are depleted. By contrast, CanRoys are set up to operate indefinitely by acquiring and replenishing reserves.

One of the great appeals of CanRoys is that much, and sometimes all, of the distribution is tax free because of flow-through depletion allowances and other deductions from items like depreciation of equipment. But the base price for the trust unit is adjusted downward as well, so there is a larger capital gain when the units are sold, if the units hold their price.

That said, CanRoys, with their double-digit dividends, perpetual asset growth model, and safe location within a secular energy bull market, makes for a fine core holding within any double-digit income portfolio.

Rapid Price Appreciation

What keeps the price of CanRoy shares appreciating is a two-fold situation.

First, as the price of oil and natural gas rises, the value of those proven reserves (not yet recovered) also rises—thereby providing for higher asset value when calculating share prices.

Second, as the trust earns more income from selling oil and gas into the spot market, the dividends naturally climb as well, effectively raising the dividend payout rate. This projected higher income stream also buttresses the share price of royalty trusts.

There are currently about 30 CanRoys trading on the Toronto Exchange. Of those 30 stocks, eight of them now also trade on the New York Stock Exchange (NYSE). It was only recently that Wall Street institutions were cleared by the Securities and Exchange Commission to own these securities. So the sector is still in the early innings of institutional accumulation.

As this market matures, we will see more of these trusts list their shares on the NYSE. Still, there are plenty to choose from for our double-digit income investing purposes. One interesting thing about CanRoys is that most of the trusts have caveats built in that don't allow foreign ownership to exceed 49 percent. This is a built-in demand driver for the sector given the limited number of listed trusts available.

When choosing which CanRoys to go with, I recommend sticking with those trusts that are expected to increase the volume of their oil and gas reserves for the next two years out. This seems to be a foundational component to the success of each of these stocks—knowing that the trusts replenish their reserves at a rate that is higher than the rate at which they are pumping out.

A Few Advantages

For many income investors, one of the most important reasons to own these securities is because they pay their dividends every month. And because they pay every month, the stocks rarely give much back on ex-dividend day. In fact, buying on an ex-dividend day can prove to be a savvy move if the stocks pull back.

Because CanRoys are considered foreign investments, there are a few special considerations you need to be aware of when it comes to taxes. Each Canadian Royalty Trust provides detailed tax information on its web site, and each differs slightly when it comes to rules and regulations.

As of November 1, 2006, there is a new tax proposal being voted on that, if passed, will begin to tax all Canadian Income Trusts at the same rate as corporations, starting in 2011. This has called into question the sustainability of the current high dividend payouts if the tax plan is passed. My view is that dividend payouts would be reduced by about 20 percent from current levels. So bear that in mind when considering CanRoys.

Some CanRoys are registered in the United States as foreign partnerships and some as foreign corporations. The Canadian government applies a 15 percent nonresident withholding tax on all distributions to U.S. citizens. So expect to see those monthly debits hit your account as separate items from the distributions themselves. But you can recover a portion of those taxes by filing for a refund when you submit your U.S. tax return. The 15 percent withholding tax rate drops to 10 percent in 2011.

Dividends from these Canadian Trusts are treated as qualified dividends, letting you keep 85 percent of your net dividend. If you are a U.S. resident and can recapture a portion of the nonresident withholding tax then that makes for a nice payday on the fifteenth of every month.

Here are seven of the Canadian Trusts traded on the NYSE that I follow in the 25% Cash Machine:

1. Pengrowth Energy Trust (PGH): 14.83 percent yield
2. Enerplus Resources Fund (ERF): 9.25 percent yield
3. Canetic Resources Trust (CNE): 15.82 percent yield

Figure 6.1
CNE Weekly

Source: DTNIQ.

4. Harvest Energy Trust (HTE): 15.47 percent yield
5. Penn West Energy Trust (PWE): 10.88 percent yield
6. PrimeWest Energy (PWI): 13.78 percent yield
7. Provident Energy Trust (PVX): 11.59 percent yield

Summing up, we have a beautifully designed income vehicle that is in an inflationary sensitive sector and that is invested in Canada where political/military/terror risk is minimal. And it pays monthly dividends that range between 10 to 13 percent that are largely tax free and meet the rigid accounting standards of the New York Stock Exchange. (See Figure 6.1 for example data.)

Some of the juiciest yields and returns that exist in the entire double-digit income universe can be found in the energy patch. There are so many reasons to own energy on a long-term basis that I almost don't know where to start. Big increases in domestic energy consumption are the result of a powerful rebound in the U.S. economy. The majority of the world's oil supplies are controlled by a handful of nations, and the situation is fraught with political and military risk. And that big sucking sound we hear coming from the Far East is the insatiable demand for oil and gas products thanks to double-digit GDP growth coming from China, India, Indonesia, and the rest of the Pacific Rim.

Income trusts are becoming increasingly popular, especially the energy, oil and gas trusts. Part of the reason for their success is that oil and gas prices have soared, and so has the yield on many of these trusts. However, with the industrialization of China, India and many other second- and third-world nations, the demand for oil and gas looks like a good long-term bet for investors. And getting 80 to 90 percent of operations paid out in the form of cash dividends yielding 10 percent+, makes a lot of sense to a lot of investors who need to beat the 4.5 percent rate of return on Treasuries and CDs.

Security Spotlight

Let's take a closer look at three outstanding examples of Canadian royalty trusts. Each of these securities would be a good fit for any double-digit income portfolio, but you must always keep in mind that circumstances in any individual security and in any given sector are always changing. That means that depending on when you are reading this, these securities may not be well-suited for your 25% Cash Machine. Still, they provide good pedagogical tools for understanding this sector.

Harvest Energy Trust (HTE)—13.9 Percent Yield as of 7/31/06

Harvest is one of Canada's largest conventional oil and natural gas trusts, actively managed to maintain or increase cash flow per unit through a strategy of acquiring, enhancing, and producing crude oil, natural gas, and natural gas liquids. Harvest's current production is

Figure 6.2
HTE Weekly

Source: DTNIQ.

weighted approximately 75 percent to crude oil and 25 percent to natural gas (see Figure 6.2).

PrimeWest Energy Trust (PWI)—10.7 Percent Yield as of 7/31/06

Also one of Canada's largest energy trsts, PrimeWest Energy engages in the acquisition, development, exploitation, production, and marketing of oil and natural gas. The company primarily operates in the Western Canada Sedimentary Basin and has a reserve life index of over 12 years (see Figure 6.3).

Figure 6.3
PWI Weekly

Source: DTNIQ.

Provident Energy Trust (PVX)—10.7 Percent Yield as of 7/31/06

Provident Energy Trust is a Calgary-based, open-ended energy income trust that owns and manages an oil and gas production business and a natural gas liquids midstream services and marketing business. Provident's energy portfolio is located in some of the most stable and predictable producing regions in Western Canada, Southern California, and Wyoming with proved plus probable oil and gas reserves of 134 million barrels of oil equivalent (see Figure 6.4).

Figure 6.4
PVX Weekly

Source: DTNIQ.

Canadian Business Trusts—"Sexy" Need Not Apply

There has been a quiet, yet significant boom in the way Canada's businesses are reshaping themselves. During the past five years, a Canadian phenomenon has seen more than 230 generally mature (and often boring) businesses with stable cash flow change their corporate structure to attract investors hungry for stable payouts in today's low interest-rate world. And in the business of income-oriented trusts, it seems the more boring a business is, the better it seems tailored for being an income trust. "Sexy" businesses need not apply.

CBTs are in businesses like cold storage, air cargo, public utility operations, timber, manufacturing, food distribution, greenhouse growing, building materials, ice production, and recycled energy. And while they don't sound very exciting, they are businesses currently enjoying strong industry-specific conditions and benefiting from long-term secular bull-market conditions.

A Little Bit of History

Before we go too far into this topic, let's look at a little of the history behind CBTs. I tend to get a better sense of something when you know its history, so here goes. The first Canadian tax ruling enabling the income trust structure was awarded in December 1985 to the Enerplus Resources Fund royalty trust. The first corporate conversion into a proper business trust (using the 1985 ruling) was Enermark Income Fund in 1995. The move attracted little attention at the time because the vast majority of trusts were still Real Estate Investment Trusts (REITs) and royalty trusts.

The trust structure was "rediscovered" after the dot-com crash of 2000, as investment banks were searching for new sources of fees after the initial public offering (IPO) market had dried up. The first high-profile conversion was the former Yellow Pages Group becoming the Yellow Pages Income Fund and raising $1 billion (Canadian) in the process. By 2002, trusts accounted for 79 percent of all money raised through IPOs in Canada, with only 38 percent in the traditional sectors of petroleum and real estate.

Then, by 2005 the income trust sector was worth $160 billion ($135 billion U.S. at October 2005 rates). The mere announcement by a company of its intention to convert could add 10 to 20 percent to its share price. Trusts received another boost in 2004–2005 as the provinces of Ontario, Alberta, and Manitoba implemented limited-liability legislation that shields trust investors from personal liability.

Partly as a result of this ruling, Standard & Poor's then announced plans to add the largest income trusts to the S&P/TSX Composite Index—which it eventually did on December 19, 2005 starting with a 50 percent weighting and gaining full representation on March 17, 2006.

Business trusts have come to the attention of the Canadian government. In the March 2004 federal budget, Finance Minister Ralph Goodale had tried to prohibit pension funds from investing more than 1 percent of their assets in business trusts or owning more than 5 percent of any one trust. Powerful funds led by the Ontario Teachers Pension Plan, which at the time had a significant stake in the Yellow Pages Income Fund, fought the proposed measure, and the government backed off and suspended the restrictions.

A Quick Review of the Pass-Through Security Concept

Let's take a minute to review a bit: Yield is the cash distribution paid to the investor, divided by the price of the income trust unit. Income trust investors (often retirees) are typically motivated by the size of the distribution rather than the potential for a capital gain or loss on the unit price. The reality is that income trusts have given many retirees cash flow that they have been unable to find anywhere else.

As a flow-through entity (FTE) whose income is redirected to unitholders, an income trust structure avoids the double taxation that comes from combining corporate income tax with shareholders' dividend tax.

If the tax regime allows it, a corporate subsidiary set up to run a trust's business pays a liability that reduces its tax bill, preferably to zero—making those payments to the trust unitholders a *pass-through taxation.*

In a typical income trust structure, the income paid to an income trust by the operating entity may take the form of interest, royalty or lease payments, all three of which are normally deductible in computing the operating entity's income for tax purposes. These deductions can reduce the operating entity's tax to nil. The trust, in turn, "flows" all of its income received from the operating entity out to unitholders. The distributions paid or payable to unitholders reduces a trust's taxable income, so the result is that the trust would also pay little to no income tax. The net effect is that the interest, royalty, or lease payments are taxed at the unitholder level.

With Everything There Are Risks

Income trusts are equity investments, not fixed income securities, and they share many of the risks inherent in stock ownership. Each trust has an operating risk based on its underlying business—the higher the yield, the higher the risk. They also have three other risk factors:

1. *Lack of diversification:* Unlike mutual funds, income trusts are generally single-sector or even single enterprises, and their investments are sensitive to business cycles, especially for real estate and commodities trusts.

2. *Potential sacrifice of growth:* Most revenue is passed on to unitholders, rather than reinvested in the business. In some cases, a trust can become a wasting asset, because many income trusts pay out more than their net income and the shareholder equity (capital) may decline over time.

   In such cases, investors are really receiving their own capital back through the distributions. According to one recent report, 75 percent of the 50 largest business trusts in Canada pay out more than they earn. When it comes to buying income trusts it is imperative that the earnings more than cover the payout to unitholders—if not, then the trust will either incur debt to maintain the dividend or give you your own money back in the form of a return of capital to help pay for the dividend. And that's not good.

   This means that income trusts do not guarantee minimum distributions or even return of capital. If the business starts to lose money, the trust can reduce or eliminate distributions. Of course, this is usually accompanied by sharp losses in the market value of the units.

3. *Exposure to regulatory changes:* While REITs and royalty trusts are generally well-established, single-company business trusts can cause significant losses in government tax revenue if they become too numerous—quite simply, the government may decide to intervene and remove some of the tax benefits.

A Few Advantages

I suspect that the growing numbers of people who are buying Canadian income securities are doing so for most of the same reasons that I am.

One of those reasons is the Canadian dollar's rise in value against the U.S. dollar. This makes Canadian trusts a "currency play" and that is attracting strong money rotation into Canadian financial assets, which in turn is providing a new, high level of visibility for income trusts by new institutional and retail investors. I also believe that if interest rates remain relatively low, pension funds will have to buy income trusts to meet their liabilities for retirees—and, of course, this will push prices higher.

Finally, prices could also be bolstered as more income trusts are included in stock market indices and thus, by definition, indexed funds are compelled to buy them. And of course, investors have been willing to assign a higher value to income trusts than comparable equities because of their unique tax structure and typically high-dividend yields.

For our purposes, given the times, CBTs are well-suited for a double-digit income portfolio provided they are in larger-cap, fundamentally strong businesses and are diversified through a basket of individual trusts. To diffuse risk, I try to stick with income trusts that carry a market capitalization of at least $300 million.

After we pay our 15 percent foreign withholding tax on distributions and exchange rates, that Canadian portion of our strategic high-income portfolio will be paying us a combined yield of better than 10 percent—with those assets invested in one of the premier currencies in the world today.

And history has usually shown that it pays to be on the side of the stronger currency. All together now, with feeling: "O Canada!"

Security Spotlight

Precision Drilling Trust (PDS)—9.7 Percent Yield as of 7/31/06

Precision Drilling Trust is Canada's largest energy services trust. Precision is the leading provider of energy services to the Canadian oil and gas industry. Precision provides customers with access to an extensive fleet of contract drilling rigs, services rigs, camps, snubbing units and rental equipment backed by a comprehensive mix of technical support services and skilled, experienced personnel (see Figure 6.5).

Figure 6.5
PDS Weekly

Source: DTNIQ.

7

Investing like a Rockefeller

I want to address an area of investing that I think is just an amazing way for us to cash in on big dividend yields and excellent growth potential. It's a sector of the market that has emerged as a truly excellent opportunity, thanks to a shift in how these once very exclusive entities, known as private equity firms, now operate.

As a Wall Street broker for more than 20 years, I was never able to offer most of my clients a way into the private equity markets, which were reserved only for the very wealthy. Everyone heard about these private pools of capital that were consistently smashing the performance of the S&P 500's return every year, but there was a catch. If a client couldn't pony up $1 million or more to get in the game, access was denied.

Fortunately, this has all changed. Now you too can invest the way the super rich do, now you can invest like a Rockefeller. You can now get access to investment pools set up in the form of closed-end funds that get special treatment from the SEC—mainly because they provide financing to thousands of companies that most of the big banks and financial institutions wouldn't touch.

Private Equity Goes Public

These private equity companies are made up of some of the smartest people in all of finance and are attracting new capital at a robust pace. It's hard to go a week in the stock market without a major story hitting the wires about a well-known company being taken private. Neiman Marcus, Reebok, and Sports Authority have are just some of the most well-known names to have gone private in recent years. Many leading private equity sponsors have raised funds for investments through what's known as Business Development Companies (BDCs).

This new class of security is an exciting way for retail investors to jump headlong into the private equity market that was once reserved for those super rich, accredited investors—investors who have at least $1 million in liquid securities and/or a $200,000 income during the past three years.

BDCs allow the average income investor to participate in the hottest financial subsector, one that's awash in capital and opportunity, while collecting dividend yields in the range of 8 to 10 percent.

Behind the Regulations

BDCs are specially regulated retail investment companies that typically make private equity-style investments in small to middle-market companies. They are primarily focused on second-tier (also called mezzanine) financing and issuing debt instruments—many with features similar to convertible bonds and convertible preferred stocks attached to the underlying common stock.

The Small Business Investment Incentive Act of 1980 was enacted to promote public investment in private companies and to also enable BDCs to compete with private venture capital enterprises. The 1980 act provided BDCs with more flexibility than the typical closed-end fund. Specifically, BDCs are permitted to issue derivative securities, use leverage and charge performance fees.

Since BDC managers (unlike other registered funds) may charge performance fees, they have greater flexibility than typical registered funds, and they can engage in more esoteric transactions with the companies in their portfolios. They are structured like closed-end funds, whose shares trade publicly on the open market. As a result, BDCs are subject to the regulatory guidelines of the Sarbanes-Oxley Act of 2002 and other public company regulations. These regulations are good for investors because they provide that little extra assurance that you get when investing in public companies versus the less-regulated world of private equity.

Here are four basic tenets of BDCs that make them attractive investments for a double-digit income portfolio:

1. *Permanent capital:* BDCs allow investors the same degree of liquidity as other publicly traded investments while providing their managers with "permanent capital" that's not subject to shareholder redemptions like open-ended mutual funds are. Open-ended mutual funds are structured in such a way that investors can only sell and buy shares directly to and from the fund itself, while BDCs are closed-end funds and don't suffer the huge redemption pressure (when the market is down) and huge investment pressure (when the market is up).

   Let's face it, with the highly illiquid nature of the assets within the typical BDC portfolio, the last thing the fund managers need is a lot of hot money jumping in and out of the fund—and usually at the wrong time. By being structured as a closed-end fund, ownership must change hands on the exchange if someone wants to sell or buy shares.

2. *Pool of new investors:* BDCs provide access to the public markets where shareholders are not required to meet income, net worth, or sophistication criteria. Retail investors may welcome this opportunity to gain access to the private equity markets through funds managed by major private equity players. In fact, BDCs are designed specifically for retail investors. Institutional investors are less likely to invest in BDCs because a higher fee is generally charged—higher than those charged by typical private equity funds.

3. *Higher fees:* Speaking of higher fees, another plus of the BDC structure is that managers may immediately begin earning management

fees on the amount of capital raised from the BDC's initial public offering—whereas traditional private equity managers can only charge a fee on those funds invested. BDC managers may double their annual management fees by borrowing funds in the amount equal to the BDC's net asset value. The point to be made here is that BDCs can calculate their management fees based on gross assets, including any borrowings. In addition, unlike traditional closed-end funds, BDC managers may charge performance-based fees similar to those of hedge funds.

4. *Mezzanine financing opportunities:* Most BDCs target middle-market debt financing deals, which are primarily focused on second-tier, or "mezzanine" financing and debt issuance. We tend to expect that this type of investment will generate current income and offer some opportunity for gains. Therefore, investors may find that BDCs serve as a relatively safe vehicle to get a big dividend yield and realize some upside.

Another reason BDC managers have jumped on the middle market is because they view the market as vastly underserved in terms of financing. Many banks shy away from these mid-sized companies because they view them as a higher risk than large institutional borrowers.

Big Yields Mean Things Are Good

As with many other pass-through securities that we're attracted to, we like BDCs that are raising their dividends as a direct result of improving business conditions. The middle market that BDCs are targeting is comprised of a huge herd of tens of thousands of companies. The BDCs we're investing in (some of which have over $8 billion in capital), control as many as 200 companies within their respective portfolios.

BDCs avoid taxes on that portion of income and capital gains distributed to shareholders because they are regulated investment companies (RIC). To maintain its RIC status, a BDC must distribute at least 90 percent of its investment company taxable income to its shareholders each taxable year.

If a BDC is performing as it should, then it should be raising new monies constantly, enhancing the yield it charges for borrowings and doing all it can to maximize internal rates of return (IRR). When I look for BDCs to include in a double-digit investing portfolio, I want them to have an IRR of at least 15 percent.

Generally, distributions by a BDC are taxable as ordinary income or capital gains, usually in the same manner as distributions from mutual funds and closed-end funds. A BDC shareholder will recognize a taxable gain or loss when the shareholder sells his or her shares. In addition, many BDCs have dividend reinvestment plans for shareholders.

Just like any other sector of the stock market, there will be winners and losers. Success in these companies rests purely on the talent of its management team. The pressure to invest fresh funds is great and the long-term winners in this sector have deft and opportunistic management teams that are aggressively putting new capital to work.

Within the growing number of BDCs now listed, five stand out to me as solid candidates for potential inclusion in a 25% Cash Machine portfolio:

1. American Capital Securities (ACAS): 9 percent yield
2. Apollo Investment (AINV): 9.02 percent yield
3. Allied Capital (ALD): 8.10 percent yield
4. Ares Capital (ARCC): 8.27 percent yield
5. Prospect Energy Corp. (PSEC): 7.05 percent yield

If you were to buy all five in equal amounts, your aggregate dividend yield would be 8.28 percent. I know that's not double-digit yield, but occasionally it's permissible to sacrifice a little dividend yield equities with the potential to climb 20 percent or more per year like many BDCs do.

In addition to the attractive, near double-digit yields, there are many good reasons to own a few securities in this sector. First, you get exposure to an avenue of investing that we know works the majority of the time. Heck, up until now we had to be rich to step onto this playing field, and how do you think the rich got where they are? I can assure you, it's not luck. It's by having access to the best methods of growing wealth. Ways the average Joe just didn't have until now.

The second reason to own BDCs is the elite gene pool of talent working for private equity firms. We want these firms to attract the best minds money can buy. A successful fund manager can take home a rock star–sized paycheck, which is fine with us as long as they are making us profits.

Another great reason to own BDCs is growth in the middle (mezzanine) financing and debt markets. This market has legs, and I fully expect it to flourish in the coming years. Also, the growth in the number of mid-sized companies in recent years has provided BDCs with a new "sweet spot" of opportunity.

The trends in the private equity marketplace are showing good visibility, which means great growth potential. Combine this with some great dividend yields and you're right on target for a solid component in your own 25% Cash Machine.

Security Spotlight

Now let's take a closer look at three outstanding examples of BDCs. Each of these securities would be a good fit for any double-digit income portfolio, but of course, you must always keep in mind that circumstances in any individual security and in any given sector are always changing. That means that depending upon when you are reading this, these securities may not be well-suited for your 25% Cash Machine. Still, they provide good pedagogical tools for understanding this sector.

Allied Capital Corporation (ALD)—8.8 Percent Yield as of 7/31/06

Allied Capital is one of the leading BDCs with total assets of more than $4 billion. ALD has paid regular, quarterly cash dividends to shareholders since 1963. The company's private finance portfolio includes investments in over 100 companies that generate aggregate revenues of more than $12 billion and employ more than 90,000 people.

This firm specializes in growth capital investments, recapitalizations, acquisitions, buyouts, note purchases, and bridge financing. It typically makes mezzanine and equity investments in middle-market companies. ALD invests in the following sectors: business services, financial ser-

Figure 7.1
ALD Weekly

Source: DTNIQ.

vices, consumer products, healthcare services, industrial products, retail, and energy services (see Figure 7.1).

American Capital Strategies (ACAS)—9.5 Percent Yield as of 7/31/06

ACAS is a publicly traded buyout and mezzanine fund with capital resources of approximately $8.4 billion. American Capital invests in and sponsors management and employee buyouts, invests in private equity buyouts, provides capital directly to early stage and mature private and small public companies and through its asset management business is a

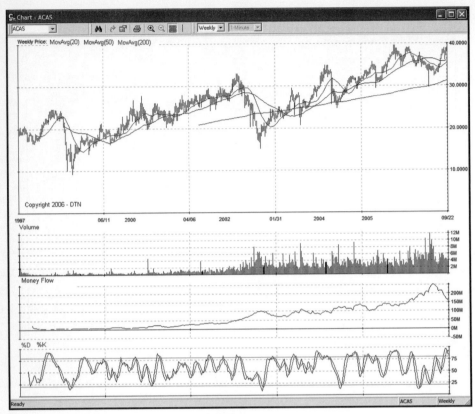

Figure 7.2
ACAS Weekly

Source: DTNIQ.

manager of debt and equity investments in private companies. ACAS invests up to $350 million per company. Since going public back in 1997,
American Capital shareholders have enjoyed a total return of 398 percent since the Company's initial public offering—an annualized return
of 20 percent, assuming reinvestment of dividends (see Figure 7.2).

Apollo Investment Corp. (AINV)—9.7 Percent Yield as of 7/31/06

Apollo Investment Corporation is a closed-end investment company
that has elected to be treated as a BDC. It invests in middle-market

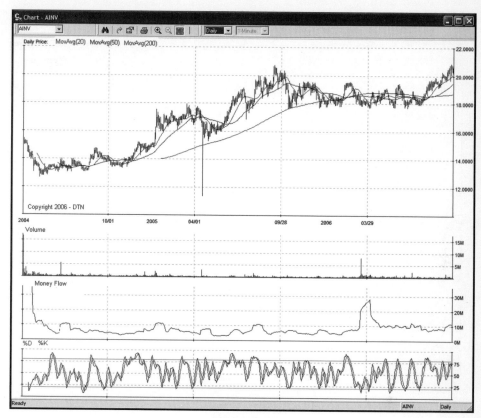

Figure 7.3
AINV Weekly

Source: DTNIQ

companies and thinly traded public companies operating in various
sectors, such as building materials, business services, chemicals, com-
munications, consumer products, energy/utilities, environmental services, financial services, healthcare, homebuilding, printing and
publishing, transportation, and media. The company was incorporated
in 2004 and has net assets exceeding $1.5 billion (see Figure 7.3).

8

Yawning All the Way to the Bank

I want to introduce you to another unique class of securities of which there are a limited number. As a class, they are referred to as Equity Income Hybrid Securities and for our purposes they can be broken down into Income Deposit Securities (IDSs). It's worth getting to know what these high-yield securities are all about.

Income deposit securities have been in use in Canada for some time but only recently debuted in the U.S. capital markets. To date, IDSs have been offered for sale by only a few restaurant industry companies, including DavCo Restaurants Inc. (the large Wendy's franchisee), Carrolls Corp. (the large Burger King franchisee and concept owner), and Buffets, Inc. (a national buffet restaurant chain).

As with any registered securities offering, the process of listing IDSs on a national exchange has made it difficult for these and other companies to successfully navigate the Securities and Exchange

Commission's (SEC) complex registration process. As a result, only a few of the offerings filed with the SEC have made it to the public market. In the case of DavCo, Carrolls Corp., and Buffets, Inc., additional investment-related issues eventually prevented these IDSs from being sold to the public.

To find quality companies and entities paying dividends north of 10 percent, you sometimes have to look outside the box and hunt for something a little more "unusual" than the typical closed-end bond fund or REIT. But this is where some good research will uncover some good ideas. Personally, I have no problem venturing into unfamiliar high-yield sectors as long as they pass muster—meaning are they earning enough money to cover the dividends and that I can expect some capital appreciation if the underlying business does well.

What's an IDS?

Essentially, IDSs and Enhanced Income Securities (EISs) are innovative securities whose underlying shares are called units—nothing new there. Units represent shares of company's common stock and debt, all combined into one security that trades like a stock on an exchange. It's a way for a company with a not-so-sexy business—like our holding in stadium concessionaire Centerplate (CVP)—to attract investors through the structuring of its stock to pay out extraordinary dividend yields.

Looking at it another way, an IDS consists of two securities (common shares and subordinated notes of the issuer) that are "clipped" together. Holders of IDSs receive dividends on the common shares and interest at a fixed rate on the subordinated notes in order to produce a blended yield. The distribution policies of IDS issuers are similar to those of REITs, MLPs, and income trusts, which distribute a significant portion of their free cash flow.

IDSs are a new type of security debuting in the United States on the American Stock Exchange (Amex). These securities are proving attractive to both institutional and retail investors, particularly in the current low-interest-rate environment. While new issues will vary, the following features and benefits will generally apply to all IDSs:

- IDSs are designed to pay a monthly income, but may also pay a quarterly dividend stream based on interest payments on the notes and dividend income, if any, on the common stock.
- IDSs are designed to distribute nearly all of a company's free cash flow to investors, allowing for the direct flow-through of any dividends and interest income to IDS holders on a monthly basis.
- IDSs are structured for issuers with mature, relatively stable businesses. These are companies well positioned in industries that are not rapidly growing, but do enjoy steady and even growth—based mostly on the sheer reality of population growth trends.

Steady as She Goes

IDSs are ideally suited to issuers that generate significant free cash flow, not high-growth companies. Industries that fit this kind of all-weather (and stable) profile include rural telephone services, dry packaged food companies, pulp mills, paper roller manufacturers, peat producers, carbon producers, phone book publishers, and commercial laundry equipment manufacturers.

We're talking about steady businesses that are not really in need of new capital to fuel growth because their businesses are already characterized by high levels of cash flow. Because these kinds of "steady-Eddie" companies grow at rates less than 15 percent per year, they don't catch the eye of most investors. By restructuring themselves as income-oriented securities that promise to pay out all available cash to shareholders, the market value of the securities themselves stands to rise in value as payouts are increased over time.

The real key of the overall IDS and EIS structure is the ability of a company to—in a systematic, predictable, and stable fashion—produce free cash flows on a capital of operating tax-efficient basis to distribute to shareholders.

Ultimately, the valuations of EIS and IDS securities are determined as a function of the credit quality and investment profile of the issuing company, the quality of its franchise in the marketplace, the stability and predictability of its cash flows, and the extent to which there is growth expected in the cash flows to increase distributions to investors downstream.

Capitalizing on the "Yawn" Factor

Canada has taken the lead in the issuance of IDSs and EISs during the past five years. The wholesale restructuring of the large number of mundane Canadian businesses into these high-powered, yielding stocks has generated more than $5 billion in legal and advisory fees for investment bankers—the equivalent of many MasterCard-sized deals.

I would expect more and more U.S. companies in equally yawn-provoking businesses that generate huge cash flow, to adopt this innovative structure to bring their companies back into the limelight. It's good for the company and it's even better for the shareholder.

There were only a handful of IDSs a few years ago. Now there are more than 150 IDSs, worth more than $60 billion trading on the Toronto Stock Exchange, with a few now listed on the Amex—and more on the way as those IDSs north of the border seek U.S. listings.

Three IDSs that I really like and that are worth taking a look at for your portfolio, are discussed next.

B&G Foods (BGF)—10.4 percent Yield

B&G Foods and its subsidiaries manufacture, sell, and distribute a diversified portfolio of high-quality, shelf-stable foods across the United States, Canada, and Puerto Rico. Products include pickles and peppers, jams, jellies and fruit spreads, canned meats and beans, spices, seasonings, marinades, hot sauces, wine vinegar, maple syrup, salad dressings, Mexican-style sauces, taco shells and kits, salsas, and other specialty food products. B&G Foods competes in the retail grocery, food service, specialty store, private label, club and mass merchandiser channels of distribution. B&G Foods' products are marketed under many recognized brands, including Ac'cent, B&M, Brer Rabbit, Emeril's, Grandma's Molasses, Joan of Arc, Ortega, Polaner, Red Devil, Regina, and Underwood (see Figure 8.1).

Figure 8.1
BGF Weekly

Source: DTNIQ.

Centerplate Inc. IDS Units (CVP)—11.3 Percent Yield

Centerplate provides catering, concessions, management, and merchandise services for approximately 130 of North America's best-known venues. CVP serves sports facilities, convention centers, and other entertainment venues. CVP operates in 10 National Football League stadiums and 6 Major League Baseball stadiums and has been contracted for 24 World Series Games, 10 Super Bowls, 8 NCAA Final Four Men's Basketball Tournaments, 14 World Cup Soccer Games, and 9 U.S. Presidential Inaugural Balls (see Figure 8.2).

Figure 8.2
CVP Weekly

Source: DTNIQ.

Coinmach Service Corporation IDS (DRY)—8.9 percent Yield

Coinmach Service Corp. is a leading supplier of outsourced laundry equipment services for multifamily housing properties in North America. Coinmach's core business involves leasing laundry rooms from building owners and property management companies, installing and servicing laundry equipment, and collecting revenues generated from laundry machines (see Figure 8.3).

Both of these IDSs companies trade on the Amex which means you can buy them through both a full-service broker or an online broker.

Figure 8.3
DRY Weekly

Source: DTNIQ.

Okay, they're not the most exciting stocks to own, but sure and steady always wins the race.

Having a couple of these highly stable sources of income in your portfolio at times when the market seems somewhat directionless provides you with a higher certainty of dividend safety and lower volatility within your total holdings.

9

Generate Income from Real Estate without Having to Own Property

Without a doubt, the real estate market has been one of the top-performing sectors for investors seeking excellent gains during the past three years. The financial returns rival those of the energy and commodities sectors, yet most investors would tell you that real estate is more conservative than the other two sectors. That's probably true from a historical standpoint, but after such a strong run, we have to be far more selective.

What I want to address in this chapter are the publicly traded securities involving pools of real estate that trade on a major exchange. These are called Real Estate Investment Trusts (REITs).

The majority of REITs are invested in brick-and-mortar assets. The income investor gets to directly invest in a diversified pool of real estate, either through properties or mortgages. REITs trade like regular common stocks and provide excellent liquidity, unlike most forms of traditional real estate.

Why REITs?

There are some obvious benefits to owning REITs. They afford the individual an opportunity to invest in commercial real estate—something that for most of us is beyond our reach. REITs also assure liquidity through stock market traded units, even though the REIT may be invested in large properties that might themselves be very illiquid. And during the recent real estate boom, REITs have performed extremely well, averaging better than 25 percent annual returns during the past three to five years.

REITs receive special tax considerations because they are structured as "pass-through securities." This simply means that in order for a REIT to receive preferential tax treatment, it has to pay out all income after operating costs in the form of a dividend to shareholders. As such, some REITs pay upward of 10 percent (and higher) on their dividend yields. By offering investors a high yield as well as a highly liquid method of investing in real estate, it's no wonder REITs are such a popular asset class.

Varieties of REITs

There are three kinds of REITs to learn about:

1. *Equity REITs:* These are the most common kind of REIT. Equity REITs invest in, and own, properties—and thus are responsible for the equity or value of their real estate assets. Their revenues come principally from property rent.

2. *Mortgage REITs:* Mortgage REITs deal in investment and ownership of property mortgages. These REITs loan mortgage money to real estate owners, or they invest in (or purchase) existing mortgages, or mortgage-backed securities. Mortgage REIT revenues are primarily generated by the interest that they earn on the mortgage loans.

3. *Hybrid REITs:* These REITs combine the investment strategies of Equity REITs with the Mortgage REITs by investing in both properties and mortgages.

Putting Your Money Down

Investors can invest in REITs by either purchasing their shares directly on an open exchange or by investing in a mutual fund that specializes in public real estate. An additional benefit to investing in REITs is the fact that many are accompanied by dividend reinvestment plans, also called DRIPs. This means you can take dividends in the form of more shares of the same REIT and compound your earnings, in lieu of taking cash payments.

Another benefit of REITs is that you can buy into a pool of real estate that targets a specific region, state, or country, allowing you to focus on the best pockets of strength within the entire real estate universe. This is ideal in that you can customize your real estate portfolio, invest in all your favorite areas, and have the portfolio professionally managed.

Show Me the Money

Let's look at the dividends that REITs pay.

The REIT dividend payment can be made up of several kinds of income: Ordinary income from rents, interest income from loans, and capital gains from the sale of properties—or even return-of-capital if that's what management feels is prudent. It follows, that with the various forms of income affecting the dividends a REIT pays out, the tax implications are just as varied.

Because REITs are required by law to pass much of their income directly to investors, they usually bypass corporate taxation, and thus, their dividends aren't eligible for the 15 percent dividend-tax rate put in place in 2003. That means investors generally pay taxes at higher ordinary income rates running as high as 35 percent.

It's understandable that some investors are persuaded to sidestep REITs as potential sources of income—out of the fear that they will be hit with larger tax bills. For this and other reasons (including the fact that investors fear rising interest rates will hurt real-estate shares), REITs have lost some of their luster.

The reality is that it is difficult to predict what category of income a REIT will pay out in a given year because the dividend amounts fluctuate sharply depending on asset sales and other variables. As mentioned earlier, some of the income that REITs pay out is in the form of "qualified dividends"—meaning they are taxable at the 15 percent dividend-tax rate. That's because the income was taxed (for whatever reason) before the REIT distributed it to shareholders.

Some income comes from capital gains, while other income from REITs is a return of capital—part of your original investment is returned to you. This kind of distribution lowers your cost basis, so you will pay capital gains taxes when you sell.

If REITs were to pay out only the income they generate from their real estate operations, then REIT investors would lose out on the lower dividend-tax rates available to other investors. But peel apart the distributions that REITs make to shareholders and you see that the payout often comes from a variety of sources—each with its own tax implication.

Here's the Deal

In closing this discussion on REITs, I want to give you several good names in this sector you can look at who are rock-steady and pay high yields.

Medical Properties Trust (MPW)—8.4 Percent Yield

Medical Properties Trust is a REIT formed to capitalize on the changing trends in healthcare delivery by acquiring and developing net-leased healthcare facilities. These facilities include inpatient rehabilitation

Figure 9.1
MPW Weekly

Source: DTNIQ.

hospitals, long-term acute care hospitals, regional acute care hospitals, ambulatory surgery centers, and other single-discipline healthcare facilities, such as heart hospitals, orthopedic hospitals, and cancer centers (see Figure 9.1).

New Century Financial Corporation (NEW)—16.2 Percent Yield

Founded in 1995 and headquartered in Irvine, California, New Century Financial Corporation is a REIT and one of the nation's premier

Figure 9.2
NEW Weekly

Source: DTNIQ.

mortgage finance companies, providing mortgage products to borrowers nationwide through its operating subsidiaries (see Figure 9.2).

Senior Housing Properties Trust (SNH)—7.2 Percent Yield

Senior Housing Properties Trust is a REIT headquartered in Newton, Massachusetts, that has $1.7 billion invested in senior living properties located in 32 states. The trend for assisted living is picking up momentum (see Figure 9.3).

Figure 9.3
SNH Weekly

Think about It!

You get all the benefits of being a property owner without having the nasty job of collecting rent, negotiating lease contracts, evicting bad tenants, repairing buildings, maintaining landscaping, and so on. Basically, investing in REITs is a liquid, dividend-paying way to participate in the real estate market.

10

Master Limited Partnerships— Not for Just the Rich Anymore

One overlooked corner of high-income paying investments is in the once-rarified air of Master Limited Partnerships (MLPs).

These are limited partnerships that are publicly traded on the security exchanges. They combine the tax benefits of a limited partnership with the liquidity of publicly traded securities.

And these babies are taxed only once at the corporate level leaving plenty of cash to pay back in the form of dividends to its shareholders.

Never heard of an MLP? That's not unusual. They don't show up on the radar screen of most individual investors.

From the outside, they look complicated. They don't get played up by the talking heads on TV. And, they suffered a big reputation hit in the

1980s and 1990s when many MLPs were involved in a number of investment scams. Secret deals. Serious debt problems. A few big partners got left holding the bag.

MLPs were once the investment playground only for the rich and big institutions. All that's changed now.

Today, MLPs have been cleaned up and have gone mainstream. Most of them are traded on the New York Stock Exchange. You can purchase shares directly from your broker. Ownership is in the form of units as opposed to shares which in effect makes you a limited partner.

Most MLPs are in oil- and gas-related businesses including energy processing and distribution. The other types of MPLs operate in a variety of businesses including coal, timber, minerals, real estate, and some in an assortment of miscellaneous businesses.

MLPs are limited partnerships whose interests (limited partner units) are traded on public exchange just like corporate stock (shares). MLPs consist of a general partner (GP) and limited partners (LPs).

Why Do I Like MLPs?

MLPs have delivered more than 17 percent annualized total returns during the last decade, leading some market analysts to forecast that the MLP sector today could be on a similar trajectory as REITS were in the late 1980s. There is the potential for tremendous growth ahead given the strong need for new energy infrastructure investment.

But I like them for four main reasons:

1. They pay a nice high yield. Usually 7 to 9 percent and most pay dividends on a quarterly basis. MLPs earnings are taxed only once, at the unit-holder level. By contrast, the earnings of most publicly traded corporations are taxed twice, once at the corporate level and once again at the shareholder level. As a result, the MLP can pay out significantly more of its cash flow to you, the unit-holder.
2. A number of MLPs are increasing their dividends. That's because many MLPs are in mature, asset-rich businesses that generate large amounts of cash flow.
3. They are relatively safe investments. Most MLPs are energy exploration and production companies, natural gas liquids businesses,

and pipelines. These businesses are not affected by the rise or fall of oil prices, and their rates are set by regulatory agencies, keeping them predictable and stable.

4. Unitholders, in turn, enjoy real tax deferment. You get enhanced distributions of cash because of the tax shelter provided by the pass-through of the noncash expenses, at a time when tax shelters are particularly hard to find. This means you will not pay taxes until it's time to sell the MLP . . . perhaps in retirement when you are in a lower tax bracket.

This tax deferment can be a big plus for investors. While the explanation behind the deferment is too complicated to go into here, it's worth noting that you will receive a separate IRS form from the partnership outlining the tax deferments making it easy for you or your tax adviser include it on your returns.

That's why MLPs are good long-term investments. You're not going to want to trade in and out of these companies.

What Do I Look for in an MLP?

First, I look for an MLP that's paying a big distribution. Most of the MLPs that I follow all pay out between 7 and 12 percent annually. Take Dorechester Minerals LP (DMLP) for one, which paid 9.50 percent this past year and is looking at a 12 percent plus forward-looking dividend.

I look at the financial strength of the partnership. In particular, I keep an eye out for debt. I consider any partnership carrying a debt-to-capital ratio below 60 percent is a safe play. Another company I follow, Energy Transfer Partners LP (ETP) carries less than a 50 percent debt-to-capital ratio while paying a growing dividend of 7.5 percent.

I also look for companies with good management. Terra Nitrogen Co. LP (TNH) fits that profile. A company engaged in the business of manufacturing fertilizer, TNH has a solid management team and a good long-term growth record. TNH has doubled its stock price over the past three years while paying out a generous 8.5 percent dividend.

And finally, I like to go with companies that are in safe and mature businesses, less exposed to the wild swings in commodities. Pipeline companies are a good example of a relatively safe bet because their prices are regulated. A good name is Valero LP (VLI), a company involved in the energy production and pipeline business with a great track record, and it pays a nice 7 percent dividend.

High-Dividend Payments and Steady Price Appreciation

Like any equity, there are risks to MLPs including lack of capitalization, changing regulatory environment, and any kind of major economic downturn.

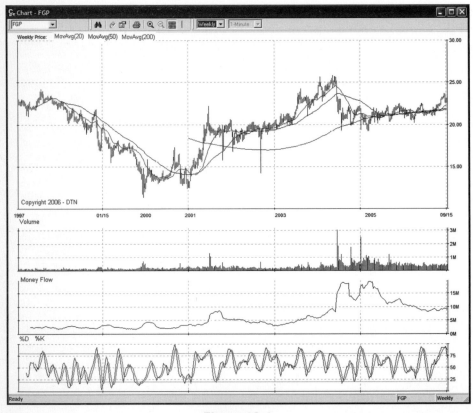

Figure 10.1
FGP Weekly

Source: DTNIQ.

Their prices could turn down if interest rates rise too rapidly. But unlike bonds, MLP prices are regulated, giving them a softer landing and slow rate of change.

One of my favorite MLPs is Ferrellgas Partners.

Ferrellgas Partners, LP (FGP)—9 Percent Yield

Ferrellgas Partners, LP (FGP) comes as close to fitting our parameters as is possible in a sector where most of the MLPs are yielding 5 to 7 percent (see Figure 10.1). FDG is unique in that it pays a tax-preferred yield of 9 percent as one of the nation's largest propane distributors—and business conditions are just beginning to improve.

So if you're looking for an investment with reasonable price appreciation while getting paid a nice dividend and with less volatility than the average large cap stock, consider MLPs.

Combined with the ability to defer tax payments, MLPs look like one investment that should be in everyone's portfolio.

11

Closed-End Funds—Not Closed at All

The growth in the issuance of closed-end funds has been nothing short of meteoric. They offer income investors multiple choices by which to ascertain various forms of income while being in highly liquid securities that usually trade on the New York Stock Exchange.

I like to think of closed-end funds as a way to buy into specific management styles that allow you to add another layer of diversification to your 25% Cash Machine portfolio of around 25 holdings. Buying a closed-end fund is buying into a basket of securities and not just one company.

More-experienced income investors are able to develop a pretty good working knowledge of convertible securities, foreign debt, and covered call writing on indexes, but most income investors don't want the angst that goes along with trying to trade those exotic markets. So we buy into proven management teams that trade these difficult markets and provide full liquidity, too, in the form of a listed stock.

Similar to common stocks, closed-end funds usually trade on one of the major U.S. exchanges. However, unlike regular stocks, they represent an interest in a specialized portfolio managed by a group of investment advisers. These managers typically concentrate on a specific industry, country, or sector.

A closed-end fund is a publicly traded investment company that raises capital through an initial public offering (IPO) and then uses the proceeds to invest in a basket of securities. Technically speaking, a closed-end fund—legally known as a "closed-end company"—is one of three basic types of investment companies. The two other basic types are mutual funds and Unit Investment Trusts. A closed-end fund is a fund with a fixed number of shares outstanding and one that does not redeem shares the way a typical mutual fund does.

Closed-end funds behave more like stocks than open-end funds (also known as mutual funds).

Closed-end funds issue a fixed number of shares to the public in an IPO, after which time shares in the fund are bought and sold on a stock exchange. They are not obligated to issue new shares or redeem outstanding shares as open-end funds are. Closed-end funds trade just as any other listed stock and subsequently shares are purchased through any type of brokerage.

The price of a share in a closed-end fund is determined entirely by market demand, so shares can either trade below their net asset value ("at a discount") or above it ("at a premium"). Conversely, an open-end mutual fund continuously offers and redeems shares based on the inflow or outflow of investors.

The purchase or sale price of an open-end fund share is its net asset value (NAV) plus or minus any load (fees) that may be applicable. NAV is the total net assets of the fund divided by the number of outstanding shares of the fund. NAV is usually not equivalent to the stock price. Most closed-end funds trade at a discount (the stock price is below the NAV) and occasionally at a premium (the stock price is above the NAV).

Closed-end funds come in many varieties. They can have different investment objectives, strategies, and investment portfolios. They also can be subject to different risks, volatility, fees, and expenses. So it pays to do a lot of comparative analysis because you will typically find dozens of closed-end funds targeting just about every investment objective imaginable.

In my view, there is a very specific benefit to owning closed-end funds over open-end funds, because there is the element of uncertainty regarding capital flowing in and out of open-end funds. Closed-end fund shares generally are not redeemable—that is, a closed-end fund is not required to buy its shares back from investors upon request.

The fund manager of an open-ended fund constantly faces a never-ending dilemma in bull and bear markets in that open-ended funds tend to attract most of their capital at the top of major bullish moves and also attract the greatest levels of selling at the bottom of major sell market sell-offs.

Open-end funds are open to new investors and can create as many shares as needed. However, closing a mutual fund to new investors does *not* make it a closed-end fund. When a mutual fund closes, it still allows current investors to buy more shares and, when those investors want to sell their holdings, they don't need to find a buyer. Closed-end funds are similar to exchange-traded funds (ETFs), but they are actively managed. (ETFs are passive, index-like funds.)

Closed-end funds, however, have a fixed number of shares. Much like a new publicly traded stock, closed-end funds have an IPO. They also trade according to market demands (i.e., every seller must have a buyer).

Here's the problem I have with open-ended mutual funds. If a fund is any good at all, it will be on the radar of millions of fund investors, willing to own it at the right time. Historically, the most money that comes pouring into mutual funds happens *after* big moves—meaning the fund manager now has to put a ton of new cash to work at the top of a major move and pay up for stocks after the easy money has been made.

Big mutual fund outflows historically occur after large percentage drops in the major averages. For example, imagine being a fund manager post-9/11 and you get a rash of redemptions as the market is opening down 15 to 20 percent across the board. In a volatile, headline-driven market—like the one we face every day where exogenous events are now more probable than possible—this can be a nightmare for fund managers as money rushes in and out of their open-ended funds, making it difficult to take full advantage of the fund's assets.

By trading in publicly traded closed-end funds, investor sentiment is factored into the price of the shares by trading at a discount or premium to the NAV.

As I said, the discount/premium relationship is primarily a sector sentiment indicator. Some of the reasons a closed-end fund may trade at a premium include heightened interest in a sector, particularly biotechnology, Internet, small-cap, and emerging markets. Conversely, if the sector or the types of securities within a fund are out of favor, it is likely that a fund will trade at a discount.

Closed-end funds also are permitted to invest in a greater amount of "illiquid" securities than mutual funds—an illiquid security generally is considered to be a security that can't be sold within seven days at the approximate price used by the fund in determining NAV. Because of this feature, funds that seek to invest in markets where the securities tend to be more illiquid are typically organized as closed-end funds.

You want to be careful if you are paying a premium over NAV for a closed-end fund. Funds that trade at premiums are holding assets considered in high demand, but that can change quickly. Keep in mind that just because a fund had an excellent performance last year does not necessarily mean that it will duplicate that performance. For example, market conditions can change and this year's winning fund could be next year's loser.

Comparison of Closed-End versus Open-End Funds

Closed-End Funds

- Diversified portfolio of securities.
- Professional management.
- Actively managed.
- Fixed number of shares issued.
- Once public, the fund is closed to new investors.
- Actively traded on major exchanges like stocks.
- Investors buy and sell shares in open market.
- Shares not redeemable through the fund itself.
- Shares can trade at a discount or premium to its NAV.
- Can own restricted or illiquid securities.

Open-End Funds

- Diversified portfolio of securities.
- Professional management.
- Actively managed.
- Nonfixed number of shares.
- Fund can create as many shares as it wants, open to new investors.
- Shares are not traded on major exchanges.
- Shares are purchased and redeemed through the fund itself.
- The purchase or sales price of an open-end fund share is the NAV plus or minus any load (fees) that may be applicable.
- Shares are always priced at NAV, no discount/premium relationship to share price.
- Can't own restricted or illiquid securities.

Similarly, if another sector of the economy is growing rapidly—like alternative energy, which competes with demand for other hot growth sectors—this too can cause a fund to trade at a discount. In this day and age, there are now millions of investors that trade in and out of closed-end funds.

They do so because it takes the risk out of owning individual stocks, yet allows them to focus investment dollars in a highly specialized portfolio with very specific objectives, including the use of leverage and derivatives like options to enhance returns. It's a bountiful buffet table out there in the world of closed-end funds and by the use of careful screening we can locate the best ones for our strategic high-income objectives.

As of early 2005, there were approximately 800 closed-end funds valued at around $371 billion. I suspect that today the number of closed-end funds has grown to over 900 with total assets in excess of $500 billion. That might seem like a lot, but it pales by comparison to the open-ended "mutual fund" industry, which boasts over 14,000 funds and total assets running into the trillions of dollars.

Here are three funds that provide a great starting point to get into closed-end funds. They all pay a nice dividend and have stable, and steady growth characteristics.

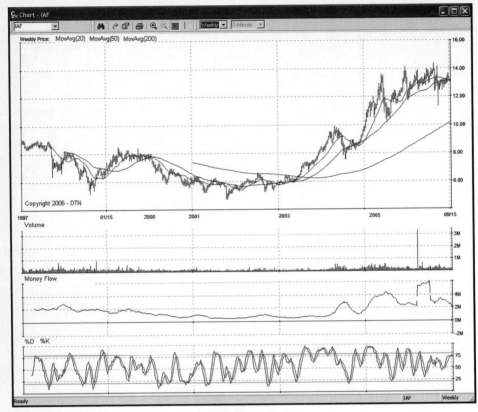

Figure 11.1
IAF Weekly

Source: DTNIQ.

Aberdeen Australia Equity Fund (IAF)—9.55 Percent Yield

This closed-end fund from Australia has assets exceeding $200 million, primarily invested in commodity stocks that have proved to be an excellent strategy. The fund has turned in an average annual return of 23.8 percent for the past five years (see Figure 11.1).

Calamos Convertible Opportunities & Income Fund (CHI)—9.1 Percent Yield

This fund seeks total return through a combination of capital appreciation and current income by investing in a diversified portfolio of convert-

Figure 11.2
CHI Weekly

Source: DTNIQ.

ible securities and below investment-grade (high-yield) fixed-income securities. The fund may be suitable for investors who are focused on long-
term total return and are looking for dynamic asset allocation to
maintain a consistent risk/reward balance throughout the market cycle
(see Figure 11.2).

Pioneer High Income Trust (PHT)—9.3 Percent Yield

This is a closed-end fund that invests primarily in sub-investment grade
corporate bonds, more commonly known as high-yield bonds. Most
high-yield funds have lost value while the Fed has raised rates for the

Figure 11.3
PHT Weekly

Source: DTNIQ.

past three years, but this one has managed to gain during this time, which is a tribute to excellent fund management (see Figure 11.3).

For your purposes, you are fortunate to have available dozens of closed-end funds trading in attractive industries that pay yields upward, or in excess of, 10 percent. By positioning some of your income assets in the right sectors paying big dividends, you can have a higher level of confidence in achieving your goal of a 25 percent annual total return.

12

Profits on the High Seas

Now, I want to scratch the surface on dry-bulk shipping and cargo stocks, as the sector is benefiting from increased trade.

For years, energy investors have sung the virtues of the double-hulled oil tanker business due to changes in the economic and regulatory climates. However, there is another side to the shipping business that is also enjoying the best of times—the dry-cargo carriers.

A lot of once-mundane industries, like these carriers, have caught fire with the emergence of China and India as the new global industrial powerhouses.

With such an explosion of first-world growth comes an insatiable demand for basic materials and energy. Given the fact that both countries produce only a fraction of what they need, the dry-bulk shipping business (where more than 90 percent of what they ship is coal, iron ore, and grain) is enjoying bull market conditions with strong long-term visibility.

The "X factor" in the business is China, clearly the biggest customer in the world.

When commodity prices or shipping rates get too high, the Chinese will simply put off purchasing or negotiating contracts until prices settle down. They have a huge influence on pricing of coal, iron ore, and grain as well as the day rates by which those items are transferred across the Pacific Ocean.

Knowing that the Chinese can manipulate the market allows us to identify our risk. Keep the long-term perspective in mind, though—China and India need coal, iron ore, and grain. Short-term periods of weakness are great times to initiate and add to the carrier positions in your portfolio.

The global economic boom, the progression of the World Trade Organization (WTO) and numerous multinational wide-reaching trading agreements have afforded the strongest of business conditions for the large-vessel dry-bulk shipping operators. As such, sales and profits are up big and so are the dividends they are paying out to shareholders.

These companies are set up as conventional S corporations but have a stated policy to pay out 100 percent of cash flow net of operational expenses to shareholders in the form of a dividend.

These dry-bulk shippers negotiate short- and long-term contracts according to current charter rates. When charter rates are up, the companies try to lock in long-term contracts. When charter rates are down, dry-bulk operators try to negotiate short-term contracts.

Three Shipping Carriers for Your Cash

I love this sector with its high yields and steady business flow, but these stocks can sometimes get a little wild on the up and down scale. It's not uncommon for some of our shipping stocks to pay 15 percent dividends but fluctuate 15 to 20 percent up or down in a given rough period. Still, here are three of my favorites that you can ride out through tough seas.

Eagle Bulk Shipping (EGLE)—14.2 Percent Yield

Eagle Bulk Shipping is the largest U.S.-based owner of Handymax dry-bulk vessels, which range in size from 35,000 to 60,000 deadweight tons (dwt), and transport a broad range of major and minor bulk cargoes, including iron ore, coal, grain, cement, and fertilizer, along worldwide shipping routes. Their strategy is to charter the company's modern fleet

Figure 12.1
EGLE Weekly

Source: DTNIQ.

primarily pursuant to one- to three-year time charters that allow them to take advantage of the stable cash flow and high utilization rates that are associated with medium- to long-term time charters (see Figure 12.1).

Frontline Ltd. (FRO)—15.6 Percent Yield

The company's tankers are used for the transportation of crude oil from the Middle East Gulf to the Far East, Northern Europe, the Caribbean, and the Louisiana Offshore Oil Port. The company's tanker fleet, the largest in the world, consists of 30 very large crude carriers (VLCCs) and 28 Suezmax tankers, as of December 31, 2005 (see Figure 12.2).

Figure 12.2
FRO Weekly

Source: DTNIQ.

Nordic American Tanker Shipping (NAT)—16.8 Percent Yield

Nordic American Tanker Shipping Limited engages in the ownership and operation of crude oil tankers in Bermuda. Its fleet consists of nine double-hull Suezmax tankers. The company operates its vessels on bareboat charters, time charters, and in the spot market (see Figure 12.3).

Fresh Meat for Double-Digit Income Investors

It's just wonderful that more and more privately held industries are unlocking their values and allowing income investors a chance to buy into

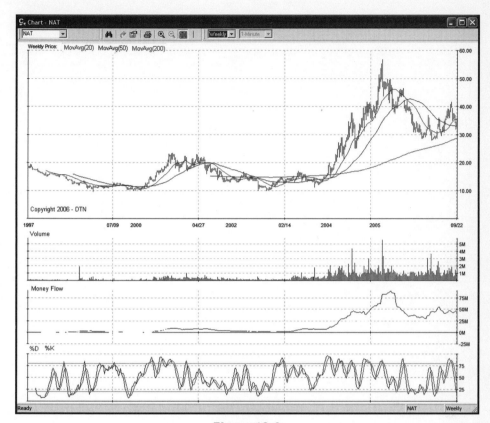

Figure 12.3
NAT Weekly

Source: DTNIQ.

these dynamic businesses that throw off phenomenal cash flows. These kinds of high-yield stocks just didn't exist 5 or 10 years ago. It really is a boon to income investors who are seeking high yields from very profitable enterprises and not just servicing below-grade debt.

Keep in mind that companies like Frontline and Eagle Bulk Shipping are paying such hefty yields because business is so good—unlike the old junk bond days when high yield meant leveraged balance sheets and companies bleeding red ink. You *can* own thriving businesses *and* get paid like a champ in the process.

PART THREE

A New Generation of Double-Digit Income Investments

13

Not All High-Yields Are Created Equal

The Declaration of Independence tells us that all men are created equal. It's a beautiful sentiment, and a bedrock principle that sets the United States apart from so much of the rest of the world. But when it comes to dividend-yielding securities, equality is definitely not written in to the investor's constitution.

In fact, just because a given security—be it a stock, a CanRoy, a REIT, or any other asset class—has an attractive dividend yield, that does not mean that it deserves a place inside the 25% Cash Machine. To be certain, a high-dividend yield is a necessary condition for inclusion in double-digit income investing. But a high-dividend yield alone is not a sufficient condition, because numbers alone don't tell the whole story.

So how do we distinguish between a good double-digit income investment and a not-so-good one? What makes one security with a 10 percent dividend yield different from another security boasting the same 10 percent return on your money? Let's find out.

The Importance of Dividend Payout Ratios

Early on in this book we introduced you to the concept of yield power. At that time, we told you that securities with yield power are those found in thriving businesses that make a lot of money. These are the securities that can afford to pay out significant portions of their cash flow to investors in the form of dividends, interest or distributions, and still have a little cash left in the tank.

Determining yield power involves a basic calculation called a *payout ratio*—the percentage of every dollar of cash flow that gets paid out to shareholders. For example, if a company has $2 of net income per share, and it pays out $1.50 of that $2, then we would say that it has a 75 percent payout ratio ($1.50 divided by $2.00 = 0.75). Another way to say it is that a company's payout ratio is a measure of how much profit it is returning to shareholders in the form of dividends.

I know it seems simple, but learning how to assess a security's payout ratio is critical to determining whether a particular security has the yield power and potential to meet the dual objectives of *both* double-digit yields and 15 percent annual growth in the value ofthe underlying asset. Not all of the holdings in a 25% Cash Machine portfolio will display these characteristics, but we want to try to have a significant portion of our portfolio positioned so that it can meet our goals.

In double-digit income investing, most of the securities we look at are structured as *pass-through* securities, meaning that they funnel most of the profits to their shareholders in the form of regular distributions. In other words, they *pass* the majority of their earnings *through* to their shareholders.

By their very design, pass-through securities are going to have abnormally high payout ratios when compared to your average stock. In fact, with the dozen or so classes of securities used in double-digit income investing, the payout ratios will run between 50 percent and 95 percent. This is drastically higher than your average blue-chip stock because blue-chip companies retain most of their earned income for organic growth purposes.

When evaluating securities for attractive yield power, you have to compare payout ratios the same way a growth stock investor might compare a company's price-to-earnings (P/E) ratio. I am sure most of you know that the P/E ratio is a key metric to determine the health of the average stock. Well, the payout ratio is the key to determining whether a security is healthy enough to make it into a 25% Cash Machine portfolio.

When selecting securities for your 25% Cash Machine portfolio, you want to find the ones that pay the highest possible yield with the lowest possible payout ratio.

Why is this so important to the objectives of double-digit investing? Because if a security's payout ratio is in the "sweet spot," meaning that it can pay a dividend yield of 10 percent or more and still have money left over to help the underlying business grow, you've just hit the jackpot. Your first objective of double-digit returns is met via the high yield, and your second objective of 15 percent annual growth in the underlying value of the asset is also much more likely to be met when a company can reinvest a hefty chunk of its earnings to expanding its business.

Ideally, we want to see our 25% Cash Machine securities pay out that double-digit yield and stay under an 80 percent payout ratio. When I research a high-yield investment, aside from those securities that are strictly designed to pay out 100 percent of net income, I want to see a payout ratio of no more than 80 percent on our pass-through securities, because then I know there is at least 20 percent of net capital going back into the business to grow it.

Comparing Payout Ratios

Before we go on with our discussion of payout ratios and how to compare them when evaluating securities, I want to tell you that unlike other metrics such as P/E ratio or dividend yield, locating the payout ratio for a given security takes a bit of digging. In the case of a P/E ratio or a dividend yield, this information can be found in numerous financial news sources such as Internet web sites and the stock tables of just about any newspaper in the country that has a decent business section.

But in the case of a payout ratio, this information is just not listed in your average stock table, nor can you just punch it up on Yahoo! Finance or CNBC.com. Payout ratio information is buried in the most recent financial statements issued by a company. It's up to you to do the calculations using the net income per share data and the per share dividend amount. Before you can do this, however, you have to be able to identify which securities to look at in a given asset class, what a typical payout ratio for that asset class is, and you have to have the time and patience to do all of the digging and calculations for yourself.

Now I suspect that some of you, having now heard that you are going to have to scour through financial statements with a calculator in hand, may feel like closing this book and just giving up on the whole idea of double-digit investing. Hey, I understand that sentiment. After all, the last thing you want to do when you are retired or approaching retirement is to have to sit down in front of a bunch of financial statements. Fortunately, there is a way for someone to do the heavy lifting for you.

In my 25% Cash Machine advisory service, I do all of the work for you when it comes to both locating specific securities in a given asset class, and doing the math to determine payout ratios. I've also had a couple of decades' experience with evaluating equities, which helps me know whether a security fits the criteria of double-digit income investing.

When comparing payout ratios, context is the key. Different securities sport very different payout ratios, and an attractive payout ratio for one asset class might be atrocious for another. For example, Canadian Royalty Trusts have payout ratios that average about 75 percent. But if General Motors had a 75 percent payout ratio, you'd be darn certain it couldn't maintain that level of dividend payment. The key here is to compare apples with apples.

In Table 13.1, we see the clear differences between the average yield and the average payout ratio of each of the listed asset classes. The average payout ratio provides us with a benchmark for determining the worthiness of a particular income security.

If I were buying a utility stock, I would want the payout ratio to be at or below 60 percent, the average for this sector. Why? Well, if the utility company is only going to be paying me an average dividend of 3 to 4 percent, then I expect for them to put a lot of money back into the busi-

Table 13.1
Payout Ratio Differences

Type of Security	Average Yield (%)	Average Payout Ratio (%)
Utility Stocks	3–4	60
Fortune 500 Companies	2–3	45
Canadian Royalty Trusts	10–12	75
BDCs	9–11	65
REITs	7–10	100
MLPs	8–12	100

ness to grow earnings and push up the price of the underlying shares. Unfortunately, these types of stocks don't usually sport the kind of price appreciation we're looking for, nor do they pay double-digit yields, which is why we don't use them in the 25% Cash Machine.

The Importance of Dividend Payout Ratios

Dividends are one way companies share profits with their investors. But companies also usually need to plow some of their profits back into the business, if they hope to modernize their production operations, fund the kind of adequate research and development to ensure a steady line of innovative products and make other improvements crucial to the longer-term success of the business.

Most of the securities that pay dividends with yields approaching 10 percent are structured as pass-through securities—they simply funnel the majority of the profits to the shareholders in the form of regular distributions. So, the kinds of securities we are investing in—and we're doing it purely by design—will have abnormally high payout ratios.

A company's dividend payout ratio is a measure of how much profit it is returning to shareholders in the form of dividends. Some companies strive mightily to increase their dividends on a regular basis—even in those periods when their earnings may actually decrease. The result is that their payout ratio will jump, if only temporarily.

Let's be sure we keep this concept in context—that's all-important here.

As far as common stocks go, utility companies tend to have the fattest payout ratios, roughly 40 percent—providing investors with a dividend yield of somewhere between 3 percent and 4 percent. An investor is well advised to compare the payout ratio of one particular company of interest with others in the same industry, in order to better understand if payout ratio is inline.

Certainly, different industries sport very different payout ratios and depends on the type of security we're talking about.

Canadian Royalty Trusts have payout ratios that average about 75 percent, which is normal for them. We wouldn't expect a company like General Motors (GM) to have a 75 percent payout ratio, since they need to reinvest in R&D, retooling, and a number of other expenses necessary to become and stay competitive. In fact, it's not a surprise that shareholders just got nailed with a recent 50 percent cut in dividends.

In the context of the dozen or so classes of securities we are investing in, the payout ratios will run between 50 percent and 95 percent because they are not your average blue chip stocks that keep most of the earned income for organic growth purposes. They are designed to kick out the majority of what they earn, ergo, they have higher payout ratios.

So, hopefully you understand how companies like the ones we follow can have payout ratios averaging between 70 percent and 95 percent—and can manage to pay out double-digit dividend yields on businesses that are showing fundamental improvement.

It's a similar situation with Fortune 500 companies. Here the average dividend yield is just 2 to 3 percent, and the average payout ratio is a just 45 percent. The reason this payout ratio is so low is because these companies use most of their earnings to help grow their businesses. With these companies, the primary concern is not the dividend yield, but the appreciation of the share price.

Now, if we're investing in an entity like a Canadian Royalty Trust, then we want to make sure that two conditions are present. First, we want to get our double-digit yield, which as you can see is well within the average for these securities. But we also want an attractive payout ratio, that is to say, one that is right around the 75 percent range. I like to say that a good CanRoy has a payout ratio of up to 80 percent. In an ideal world, the lower the payout ratio the better, assuming of course that you still get your double-digit yield.

It's a similar situation with BDCs. They too pay double-digit yields, but their payout ratios are high compared to other asset classes such as common stocks. In the case of BDCs, we also want to find the ones with no more than an 80 percent payout ratio. That 20 percent left in the tank to help grow the business and help move the underlying value of the security higher is the key component to meeting our objective of capital appreciation in the 25% Cash Machine.

Now the exceptions to finding securities with a bit of juice left in the tank are REITs and MLPs. If we are investing in these, like we often do, then I want a 100 percent payout ratio. That is the standard for this kind of investment, as they are designed to pass through all of their income to shareholders.

Look at it this way; if we're going to get two to three times the dividend yield of common stocks, then we would naturally expect the payout ratios to be much higher. Sure, ideally, we want to see our high-yield growth stocks pay out a double-digit yield and stay under an 80 percent payout ratio. But with some asset classes that is not possible.

Watch Out for Return of Capital

In the hunt for elephant-sized dividend yields, you've got to be careful you don't get trampled by those rogue equities out there that simply give you back your original investment.

The beasts we are talking about here are stampeding their way to double-digit yields through a practice known as "return of capital," and for the most part, it's not what you want to have happening to your money. Yield-hungry investors must always be wary of how a company is paying out its big dividends, not just aware that they are paying big dividends.

It's almost as if to be a good double-digit income investor, you have to first put on your skeptic's hat. You have to constantly question how a company can afford to pay out that big dividend, and not just accept the fact that a high-dividend exits, and that therefore everything is co-pasetic with that investment.

To understand what I mean when I say return on capital, we go back to the concept of payout ratios. If a security's payout ratio exceeds 100 percent of earnings, it tells us that the company simply isn't making enough profit to cover its stated dividend.

Instead of cutting the dividend and running the risk of chasing away shareholders, the company maintains the dividend payout at the higher level and essentially pays the difference out of cash reserves. I know, this practice of deficit financing sounds like what so many Americans are doing with their own personal finances, but it's not wise for them to do so, nor is it a wise practice for companies trying to cling to shareholders.

The trouble with this return of capital situation is that—aside from a negative payout ratio that leaves zilch in the tank for growth—these companies are going to lower the cost basis on your shares by whatever fraction per share their shortfall is. How will you know what this difference is? Well, you'll see it on your year-end tax statement from the company.

The pernicious result of this practice is that when you go to sell your shares down the road, you will pay a higher capital gains tax because your cost basis has been lowered due to the return of capital payments as part of those past, artificially pumped up dividends.

Given this situation, why do companies employ this practice of return of capital? The answer is simple: They want to keep their dividends constant during bad times, and they are counting on being able to recover organic growth of their dividends (at some point in the future) in order to cover 100 percent of the payout. The danger is that if a company continues this process of return of capital for an extend time; your cost basis can eventually fall to zero.

This is a particular concern with nonrenewable domestic energy trusts, where there is a fixed-dividend policy in place along with a rapidly depleting base of resource assets. In this situation, we would see a rising percentage of dividend payments in the form of return of capital as the trust ages toward total depletion. You don't have this situation with CanRoys because they are allowed to acquire more resource assets. This difference between domestic and Canadian energy trusts is one reason why CanRoys have become so popular in recent years.

In my 25% Cash Machine advisory service, I am always watching my recommended securities for any hint of the return of capital problem. One way to make sure you aren't going to get yourself in this situation is to select securities with relatively low payout ratios when compared to others in their class.

Show Me the Money Flow

It is relevant in any investment thesis to consider whether there is something called "institutional interest" at work. In my view, this is an important component to the overall trading landscape of any security. You simply want to know that fund managers with deep pockets are attracted to the same names you are. Measuring this "money flow" is important when determining a good double-digit income security from a not-so-good one.

The reason for this is that the big institutional money moves markets. It's not you and I buying and selling securities in our retirement accounts that make a stock, CanRoy, REITs, and other instruments climb in value. Rather, it's the big fund managers at Fidelity, Merrill Lynch, Goldman Sachs, and other institutional giants that buy shares in BIG blocks that make the value of a given security rise.

In my office, I have eight 20-inch computer monitors set up to keep track of about 300 high-yield securities. One reason I have all of this information in front of me is so that I can see, and measure, the money flow throughout the day in the various income assets that I manage.

By looking at all of these computer screens at once, I can see where the big money is flowing to, and where it is flowing from. In double-digit income investing, it's very important to assess this money flow because you want to be in securities that are attracting big money flow over time.

Here again, determining money flow is not an easy task for the average investor. You have to come to the table with a lot of knowledge and a lot of equipment to properly determine institutional buying. There are some sources of this information out there; it's scattered and not easy to locate on your own. A big part of what my 25% Cash Machine advisory service provides is a constant watch on money flow in all of the various income securities appropriate to double-digit income investing.

Wrap Up

To find quality securities paying dividends north of 10 percent, and that have the potential for a 15 percent annual bump in the value of the underlying assets, we have to look to the new and exciting asset classes that have made their way on to the investment playing field in recent years.

However, knowing which securities to choose from can be difficult, because not all dividend-paying securities are created equal. That is where the knowledge of determining yield power through the proper analysis and comparison of payout ratios comes in. Make no mistake, this process can be arduous and time consuming, but I assure you that if you are willing to do your homework, you will be handsomely rewarded with excellent yields and outstanding growth. If you prefer to have someone help you with this homework, the 25% Cash Machine advisory service is there to assist you.

So, we've now learned how important payout ratios are when evaluating a double-digit income security. We also now have our list of asset classes to choose from that provide us with the opportunity to achieve the objectives of the 25% Cash Machine. But just selecting some high-quality, high yield power securities and hanging on to them forever isn't enough.

In addition to picking the right securities, you have to know when to buy, and when to sell them. You see, the 25% Cash Machine is not just a buy-and-hold form of investing. This strategy requires some movement in to, and out of, certain market sectors from time to time. How often and under what conditions? That is what we'll find out in the next chapter.

14

Dynamic Sector Rotation

My ChangeWave colleague Tobin Smith has a great line that he often uses when debating someone on the merits of a particular equity. He'll say, "Right idea, wrong stock." Basically, Tobin is acknowledging the validity of the reasoning process behind his opponent's opinion, while at the same time saying that this reasoning process just doesn't apply in that particular situation.

Let's borrow Tobin's great line for a minute, but this time we'll put our own double-digit income spin on it. When it comes to selecting securities for inclusion in the 25% Cash Machine, you want to have the "right idea, right time."

You see, it's not enough to just know how to identify good high-yield securities sporting attractive payout ratios within one of the many new income-generating asset classes available today. In other words, you can't just have the "right idea." Once you find those good securities you'll have to step back and ask yourself whether it is also the "right time" to buy that particular security. In some cases, the answer will be an emphatic yes. Other times that answer will be a definite no.

The key here is to have a sound method for determining which sectors are strong and likely to remain strong for some time; and which sectors are weak and likely to continue down that feeble path. Once you know where the market's strengths and weaknesses are, you can then move your money in and out of these sectors to take full advantage of conditions in that market. This process of moving our money around according to market conditions is called *dynamic sector rotation,* and it is one of the key elements of double-digit income investing.

Before we get into the details of dynamic sector rotation, I want to first tell you that double-digit income investing is not some kind of difficult trading strategy that requires you to spend your retirement years in front of a computer monitor all day long. You are not going to be calling your broker regularly, making trades every day, every week, or even every month. In fact, after your initial transformation from low-yielding portfolio to 25% Cash Machine, the maintenance required on your money will be minimal.

Pick Your Spots

Most of the securities we'll be buying and holding in our 25% Cash Machine portfolio can be considered stocks with serious yield—yet, stocks nonetheless.

Any professional trader will tell you that a good trade bought incorrectly becomes an investment—and we should determine that every investment purchase should be treated as seriously as any short-term trade, where price execution is paramount. Chasing stocks demonstrates a lack of discipline—so we have to avoid getting caught up in the hype of the moment.

Most of the stocks I talk about are generally priced under $40 per share, therefore a couple of points can mean a big difference on our total return. If we are already getting an average of 10 percent on our dividends alone, and we can time our entry points correctly, making 25 percent on a combined rate of 10 percent dividend yield and 15 percent appreciation is definitely doable. But we gotta buy 'em right!

*Before you go and toss out a market order on the latest high-yield rec-
ommendation, pay attention to my buy under advice to see if you're playing according to the* squirrel monkey theory. *Don't hurry—be disciplined.*

What's the squirrel monkey theory? Glad you asked!

*The squirrel monkey is the smallest of all the primates and therefore has
the ability to climb to the highest point in a tree and crawl out onto the
smallest branches to gather the last nut no other monkey can reach.*

*But, the easy money is made by collecting the low-hanging fruit, that is,
when prices have pulled back. Have patience when positioning your stocks.
Don't be a squirrel monkey.*

Another thing you will never have to do in double-digit income investing is to try and time the market. Dynamic sector rotation does not
involve buying or selling specific equities or market segments right at
the point where their price breaks above or below a specific technical
trend line. Looking at price charts all day to determine where your retirement dollars should go is not what double-digit investing is all about.

But while double-digit income investing is not a trading strategy or
a market timing methodology, it is also not a static, buy-and-hold
strategy that requires absolutely no thought or effort after the initial
purchase of a security is made. Building a properly functioning 25%
Cash Machine isn't as easy as selecting a high-yielding dividend stock
and just forgetting about it. Hey, I would love it if this were the case,
because then once I went through all of the steps involved to identify
the good investments from the bad, I'd be set. My work here, as they
say, would be done. Unfortunately, reality dictates that we do it another way.

You see, we simply cannot escape the dictums of reality, and one of
the realities of markets is that they are constantly in flux. Business conditions in any every sector of the market change with time. Some sectors may have a slower rate of change than others, but nevertheless, the
prevailing winds of change blow continuously over the entire investment landscape.

Dynamic sector rotation is a technique that acknowledges the changing nature of markets, and it's a tool we use to harness the power of

those winds of change. Now let's look at just how this financial wind-mill works.

Don't Get Stuck in the Mud

I've managed a lot of money for a lot of people over the past two decades, but it never ceases to amaze me how so many intelligent, pro-ductive, and otherwise rational individuals make the same mistakes over and over again with their money. One of the biggest problems, as I see it, is the belief that just because a security or market sector has done well in the past, that somehow this means that it will do well in the fu-ture. Conversely, just because a market sector hasn't done well in the past, doesn't mean that it won't do well in the future. Have you heard that saying, "everything old is new again"? Well, that saying certainly ap-plies to the equity markets.

Perhaps the best recent example of people clinging to the belief that past performance leads to future performance took shape at the turn of the twenty-first century, in a seminal event in market history known as the Internet boom—and subsequent bust. When I think back to those days, I'm struck by how so many investors got caught up in thinking that the Internet and the new technologies that supported it were im-mune to the both the laws of economics, and to market psychology.

During the height of the Internet boom, investors were scooping up shares of just about anything technology related. Now I am not just talk-ing about novice investors hoping to hit it big in one or two stocks. I am talking about experienced, income-oriented investors who thought they could move their money into technology shares and get that much-needed kick in their portfolios that they weren't getting from traditional income securities. Many of these investors moved their money into the tech sector thinking that it just couldn't go down.

Well, we all know what happened next. Technology stocks fell, and they fell really hard. Many experienced income-investors lost a lot of money as a result of the busted technology bubble. But do you know what the worst part is? Many of those same investors out there have still not recovered from the bear market of 2000–2002. Why? Well, because instead of getting their money out of technology stocks, and even out of stocks completely, they clung to their technology stocks on the false premise that just because a stock or market sector has done well in the past means that it will do well in the future. Sadly, there are still many investors out there—maybe even a few of you reading this right now— still holding massive losing positions in stocks like Microsoft, Intel, or Cisco Systems that you bought at or near their all-time highs.

I tell this little cautionary tale because it illustrates two very important lessons about investing. First, you never want your money to get stuck in the mud like so many investors did just a few short years ago. You don't want to cling to the premise that these stocks will come back "eventually." Markets are constantly in flux, and the sooner you realize this, your whole approach to investing will change.

The second lesson is that to avoid getting stuck in the mud, you have to employ a strategy that enables you to identify the market sectors that are weak, and that must be avoided. The flipside to this is that the same strategy that helps you avoid weak sectors must also help you identify and act on the sectors that are showing strength. After all, you can't just successfully avoid market weakness and say "mission accomplished." You have to also be able to pick winning, double-digit yielding securities in the "right place, right time." And that's what dynamic sector rotation is all about.

Digging into the Details

Success from the 25% Cash Machine relies on a lot of parts working in conjunction with each other to produce the desired objectives of double-digit dividend yields and capital appreciation on the order of 15 percent per year. We've covered many of these mechanisms in the first seven chapters, including how to identify companies with attractive payout ratios that are spinning off 10 percent or more per year in profits to investors. One of the reasons why these companies are able to pay double-digit dividends and still have some cash left in the tank to fuel growth is because they are in industries with favorable business conditions.

Unlike guaranteed securities such as CDs, money market funds, and Treasuries, the instruments we use in the 25% Cash Machine are actual enterprises that generate profits from their various business activities.

Whether it is CanRoys, BDCs, REITs, or dividend-paying stocks, the securities we choose in double-digit investing are all subject to the prevailing conditions in their specific market sector.

If market conditions are favorable in a given sector, the securities within that sector are much more likely to perform the way we want them to. Conversely, if conditions in a given market sector are not favorable to companies in a particular industry, it doesn't really matter how good or how well-run an enterprise a specific company may be—it will be hard for them to do really well. And by really well, I mean paying high yields while the share price appreciates.

Dynamic sector rotation first entails identifying the areas of the income-asset world where business and economic conditions are favorable, and of course, where they are unfavorable. After we've identified the good from the bad, we can overweight our portfolio in the sectors with the greatest potential for continued growth, and we can minimize or eliminate our exposure to those areas where conditions are not conducive to achieving our objectives.

In the past couple of years, the fundamentals in the energy sector have been overwhelmingly favorable for income investors. Just about every piece of news that hit the energy sector in 2005 and 2006 was positive from a supply and demand standpoint. A voracious demand worldwide for oil, and the prospects for this demand growing almost exponentially in the coming decade as a result of the industrial resurgence in both China and India has sent the demand side of the equation soaring.

On the supply front, 2006 saw all-time high prices for a barrel of crude oil. We witnessed geopolitical turmoil in many of the Middle East countries that produce the lion's share of the world's oil, and continued military conflict in Iraq and its neighbors have not only caused the price of oil to spike, but it has also caused fears that supplies will be restricted in the future. Heightened demand for oil and restricted supply equal big profits for companies whose main focus is getting that black gold out of the ground.

Now with all this in mind, it is no wonder that in 2005 and 2006, energy sector securities outperformed the market at large. Savvy income investors were able to profit mightily from securities with exposure to this sector, namely, CanRoys. So it should come as no surprise that over the past year or so, my 25% Cash Machine advisory service has maintained an overweight position in energy in general, with a particular emphasis on CanRoys.

This is a prime example of dynamic sector rotation at work. By identifying favorable business conditions in the oil market, we were able to allocate our capital to securities that perform well under the prevailing market circumstances.

Personally, I don't see the supply and demand equation in the energy sector changing drastically anytime soon, but that doesn't mean that it couldn't change. As investors you always have to be prepared to make moves that maximize your chances of success. With that in mind, if oil sector fundamentals break down and the supply and demand equation reverses direction, we won't hesitate to reduce our holdings or even eliminate our exposure to CanRoys.

Harnessing the Changewave Alliance

It's one thing to know a lot about the fundamentals of the energy sector. I mean let's face it, all one has to do is watch TV, read a newspaper occasionally, or just stop at the local gas station and you'll know that Middle East turmoil continues and energy prices remain exorbitantly high. But not all market trends are that easy to spot. In fact, most market trends are hidden, and most can only be identified after they've already taken shape.

From an investment advisor's perspective, identifying market trends after they've already come into public view is often much too late. Smart investors want to identify trends before they hit the mainstream; that way you can take positions in securities right before they make their really big moves to the upside. You can also rotate out of, or stay away from certain market sectors where there is bad news on the horizon. But how is this possible? How can we possibly identify with any degree of certainty what will happen in a given market sector before it actually happens? Enter the ChangeWave Alliance.

The ChangeWave Alliance is the independent arm of ChangeWave Research that allows me to assess, with a great degree of confidence, the trends in the market most likely to affect the income security assets that I use in my 25% Cash Machine advisory service. As of 2006, the Alliance was comprised of nearly 8,000 members, and each member of the Alliance is a decision maker and/or professional working in one of many business areas that ChangeWave Research monitors constantly. And when I say constantly, I am not exaggerating.

Nearly every week Alliance members are surveyed to get their take on the future prospects for the economy at large, as well as for the future prospects in a particular industry or market sector. The results we obtain from these surveys are nothing short of remarkable.

Alliance members tell us what their companies are likely to spend their capital on going forward, where they are likely to spend that capital, and to what degree they will spend it. They also tell us about their own personal spending, energy consumption, financial decisions, product choices, et cetera. In fact, anything we want to find out concerning a potential trend in the economy and the markets can usually be determined by surveying Alliance members.

By having this independent research arm at our disposal, we are able to spot trends in the market before they actually hit the mainstream. Now when I use the term independent to describe the Alliance, I am referring here to the differences between the ChangeWave Research firm and your typical research arm of a Wall Street investment bank. You see, far from being independent, Wall Street research firms have banking relationships with many companies in a given market sector. Those relationships often cloud the research produced by these investment banks, making their results less-than-objective. ChangeWave Research is different. We don't have any investment banking relationships muddying the waters we wade through. We don't have a vested interest in a particular market or company outcome. We just want to find out, objectively, what the trends will be so that we can take the appropriate action.

By now you can probably see how vital this objective research is to our strategy of dynamic sector rotation. If the research we get from the ChangeWave Alliance tells us that business conditions affecting a given market sector will be favorable, then we will have to strongly consider entering that sector in search of double-digit returns. If, however, the Alliance tells us that business conditions are adverse in a given market segment, then we will either avoid that sector entirely, or if we are already invested in that sector, we will rotate out of it and move our money into the sectors that offer a better chance to achieve the objectives of double-digit income investing.

Wrap Up

I know what some of you might be thinking right now. You might be thinking that in order to build a functioning 25% Cash Machine you'll need to have access to the ChangeWave Alliance. Well, certainly access to the ChangeWave Alliance will give you a tremendous edge in the battle for high yields and high growth. But for most of you direct access to the Alliance isn't possible. Fortunately, you can all have direct access to the 25% Cash Machine service, which in addition to the Alliance information, you get all of the analysis and strategy that is double-digit income investing.

Hey, there are ways to get a lot of the information you need to build a functional 25% Cash Machine on your own without the help of ChangeWave or my advisory service. It will take a lot of digging and a lot time, but it can be done. I think it's probably a lot more efficient to let us do the heavy lifting for you, but this is something you'll have to determine for yourself. The important thing is that you learn the principles of double-digit income investing, and that you integrate those principles in to your own financial strategies.

All right, we've now arrived at the point where we need to actually build our 25% Cash Machine. We now know the components, and much of the strategy involved. The only thing left to do now is figure out, in practical terms, how to actually get started, and that's exactly what we're going to do.

15

The Benefits of Double-Digit Income Investing

You've now collected just about all of the raw materials you need to begin building your very own 25% Cash Machine. You are now very familiar with many of the new investment vehicles out there that make double-digit investing possible—CanRoys, REITs, BDCs. You've also learned about some of the concepts and techniques regarding how to use many of these new high-yielding investment tools in an income-generating portfolio—evaluating payout ratios, dynamic sector rotation, and using objective research.

The next steps you need to take are more practical in nature. The action items we'll be going over soon will help you transform a low-yield, twentieth-century income portfolio into a high-yield, high-growth, twenty-first-century portfolio dynamo. But before we get into the details of just what steps you must take to get on the double-digit investing path, I want to cover a few of the advantages that come with owning a properly functioning 25% Cash Machine.

I am a firm believer in making commitments in life. I think that if you want to achieve success or if you want anything you do to turn out the way you want, you simply have to make a full commitment to that endeavor. Whether it is career, marriage, learning a new skill, maintaining good health, or managing your money according to a certain investment philosophy, one of the key ingredients to success is a full embrace of that activity.

We all know, however, that an ardent and continued commitment to anything can sometimes be difficult to stick with, particularly if we are not fully convinced that what we're doing is going to net us the results we desire. The only thing that is going to provide you with the tenacity and persistence required to stick with any commitment you make is the confidence that what you are doing will give you the payoff you desire in the end.

Think about that for a moment. Isn't the confidence that we'll achieve our desired result of increased wealth the reason why we subject our money to the risks of the market in the first place? Now with that sentiment in mind, let's look at some of the benefits that double-digit investing can provide. By doing so, we'll reinforce the reasons why you are building a 25% Cash Machine—and that will give you the confidence necessary to make the double-digit income investing commitment.

Income Streams and Diversity

The first and perhaps most basic benefit of double-digit investing is that it generates a consistently high monthly and quarterly income stream from your existing investment capital. Now at first glance this fact may seem no different than every other income-investing strategy out there. And while it is true that most dividend-oriented investment portfolios contain stocks, bonds, mutual funds, and other financial instruments that pay dividends on a regular basis, not too many of these portfolios are designed specifically to generate a 10 percent annual dividend yield.

The fact that you will only be purchasing income-oriented securities designed to pay out double-digit dividends each month and/or quarter ensures that you are going to get the income you require to pay for life's everyday expenses. Food, clothing, housing, healthcare, utilities, entertainment—all of these are everyday, out-of-pocket expenses that can easily be covered with the income you generate from a smooth running 25% Cash Machine portfolio. In most cases, the income you generate from double-digit investing will be more than enough to cover your everyday expenses without ever dipping into your principal.

The second benefit of double-digit income investing is that it offers you protection from a constantly changing marketplace. In Chapter 14, we told you that one of the primary components of the 25% Cash Machine was the ability to first identify and then to move our money into sectors of the economy where business conditions are most favorable. Of course, this also includes the ability to move our money out of those sectors where business conditions are weakest, or where our money isn't likely to achieve our dual objectives of 10 percent annual dividend yield and 15 percent annual growth.

This process of dynamic sector rotation not only helps maximize your double-digit income returns, but an ancillary benefit is that it allows you to avoid those areas of the market where your money could be in the greatest jeopardy.

Another benefit of double-digit investing that is somewhat related to the concept of dynamic sector rotation is diversification. Now I know you've all heard that building a diversified investment portfolio can help you mitigate the normal ebb and flow that takes place in the financial markets. And while it is true that diversification is important in nearly every investment strategy, the beauty of it in the 25% Cash Machine is that it is diversification within the selection criteria of double-digit investing.

For example, a normal diversified retirement portfolio may contain a high allocation to Treasury and other bonds, a medium-sized allocation to cash and a small allocation to traditional dividend-oriented stocks. That's all fine, unless of course Treasury bonds, cash, and dividend stocks are paying only single-digit returns like they have in recent years.

The diversification within a double-digit investing portfolio starts with the ability to select from a wide variety of new income-oriented asset classes, all producing significantly higher yields than a traditional diversified retirement portfolio. Because these new asset classes have exposure to a huge variety of different market segments—energy, real estate, private equity, and many other sectors—we have our own built-in version of diversification.

Additionally, because we use dynamic sector rotation to move our capital out of a given sector when market conditions dictate, we will never find ourselves getting bogged down in any one particular area of the market. There are simply too many viable options when investing the double-digit income way for you to worry about getting stuck in a market that keeps you from achieving the monthly income you require.

Smoothing Volatility and Enjoying Peace of Mind

One thing that drives nearly every investor crazy—with the possible exception of those gambling junkie day-traders—is market volatility. You know those times when the market surges higher with a huge bout of buying, only to be down with equal fury the very next trading day. One week equities look like there's no stopping them, the next week they get slapped down hard by a big angry bear paw. Well, one of the interesting benefits that come with a double-digit investing is that the securities that make up a typical portfolio are much less volatile than your average stock.

I've seen it countless times in the double-digit income portfolios that I manage for clients, and in the 25% Cash Machine advisory service model portfolio. In fact, the pattern is so noticeable it almost borders on the predictable. That is, during times when the market is sustaining heavy damage, and when the rest of the market is getting clobbered, the double-digit income portfolio remains largely on an even keel.

The Dividend Cushion

Some of the feedback I get from double-digit income investors has to do with the way these high-yielding stocks trade. They tend to trade independently of the broader market, sometimes lagging on big up days for the major averages. Let me lend you some insight as to how these strategic high-income stocks trade.

When the market is in rally mode, money will flow out of defensive stocks, like those paying big dividends, and rotate into higher PE growth stocks that are more inclined to be bid up purely on the prospect of earnings power. Conversely, when growth stocks get hammered, big paying dividend stocks tend to hold the fort, pulling back only a fraction compared to their nondividend paying sector cousins.

The high-yield income stocks will usually make a move higher based on increasing cash flows and higher dividends declared on those higher cash flows. They also make a move higher when the underlying asset enjoys a huge pop, like that of crude oil. But these income stocks are designed to pay income first and appreciate second.

When you have a $30 stock paying out $3 in dividends, you are half way home to beating the S&P 500 every year. So expecting a $30 stock to move two or three points over the course of a year isn't really asking that much, at least in my view. And you also know that your first 3 points, or 10 percent, of downside is covered by the dividend.

The goal is to be in a security that accomplishes the primary objective of paying out an exceptional yield, being in an asset class that is exhibiting strong fundamentals in those economic pockets of strength where we can expect strong money flow into those classes of securities we own. If you do those very things, the stock's prices will take care of themselves and you'll ring the register.

Now, I am not to claiming that on those really big down days where the Dow Jones Industrial Average is off 150 points that the securities in the 25% Cash Machine portfolio won't also take a hit. They are not totally immune to the general market's influences. But what does happen is that on most firmly negative days, or even just sort of moderately negative days for stocks, double-digit securities tend to hold their value very well by comparison.

One reason for this lack of downside in the 25% Cash Machine securities relative to the rest of the market is because investors in these securities know that no matter what happens with growth stocks, tech stocks, small-caps, biotech, and others, their securities will continue paying double-digit yields. And let me tell you something right now, hanging on to a security when everyone else is selling is a lot easier to do when you know you that security is spinning off a 10 percent dividend each year. It's the high P/E growth stocks that are the ones with the most volatility, and that's largely because they have no appeal other than their share price appreciation.

Institutional Impact on High Yield

It is relevant in any investment thesis to consider whether there is what is called institutional interest *at work.*

In my view, this is an important component to the overall trading landscape of any stock. You simply want to know that fund managers with deep pockets are attracted to the same names you are so as to invite money flow.

The high-yield markets of today are not the high yields of the past 10 or 20 years. Once they were dominated by highly leveraged balance sheets and junk bond ratings. But now the high-yield market is now made up of more than 20 different classes of securities that are ringing up yields that are twice those of banks and brokerages, all based on improving fundamentals.

Just last year institutions were cleared to purchase Canadian Royalty Trusts and we have seen sizable increases in trading volumes associated with their involvement. Importantly, rising volumes mean more liquidity, which in turn attracts bigger investors.

And institutions need a high level of liquidity so as to be able to enter and exit stocks without influencing the price too much.

Most of today's nonfixed income high-yield stocks are special forms of pass-through securities, whereby the shareholder receives the majority of the net income in the form of dividends or distributions. It's just like holding a basket of growth stocks with a 10 percent yield and this investing philosophy is becoming more widely accepted by institutional investors seeking better returns than those in the low single digits.

In a world where the best guaranteed rates are 5 percent, many, if not most, professional income managers simply must do better. After paying income taxes and adjusting for inflation, that same 5 percent becomes a 2 percent net—and 2 percent just ain't gonna get it for most income fund managers.

Now that the Fed looks like it is done raising rates, those asset classes that make up a strategic high-income portfolio should see strong capital inflows in the months and years ahead. Especially as more fixed income capital finds its way into higher yielding derivative securities.

Of course, when stocks are on fire and just soaring up into the stratosphere, the majority of our high-yielding, double-digit securities are generally not going to jump as high as the more volatile market sectors like those aforementioned high P/E growth stocks. However, if we do our homework properly and position our portfolio's in sectors with favorable business conditions, we can get a very good jump up in the value of the underlying securities, along with those double-digit yields.

The ability to sit back, relax, and watch the market crumble while you still collect those healthy, double-digit dividends each month contributes mightily to what I consider the number 1 benefit of a well-built 25% Cash Machine: Peace of mind.

The last thing that you want as an income investor is to lose sleep at night because you are worried about making sure you have enough monthly income to live your life the way you want to. You also don't want to worry about getting caught in a general market selloff that drags your portfolio, and your lifestyle, down to a lower level.

By employing the techniques of double-digit investing, you'll have the peace of mind that goes along with knowing that your money is working for you all of the time. Both as an income generation tool and as a tool designed to pump up your overall assets by 15 percent per year.

Finally, when you build a 25% Cash Machine, the extra bump you get in the underlying assets along with those high yields you're banking each month give you another kind of peace of mind, and that is the feeling of being able to deal with unforeseen events.

As we've already seen with my friends Caren and Dr. Jones, tragedy can strike at any time. Unfortunately, that is just the way the world works. I wish it weren't like this, but wishing for something does not make it so. The only way you can feel like you have any control at all to unforeseen negative events such as a serious illness, death of a spouse, natural disaster, or any number of financially and emotionally debilitating scenarios is to be prepared.

If you are in a position to confront and deal with a crisis, you can be objective and calculating about forming a solution. If, however, you are unprepared to deal with a crisis financially, then chances are your emotions will cloud your judgment and you'll be forced into taking action you might not otherwise take had you been better prepared.

Dealing with life's uncertainties requires peace of mind, and peace of mind is what you get when you have a properly functioning 25% Cash Machine working for you.

Wrap Up

I hope by now you're convinced that the overwhelming benefits of double-digit investing are worth the commitment it will take to learn how to build and properly operate your very own 25% Cash Machine. Like I said at the beginning of this chapter, the only thing that will keep you committed to any endeavor is the confidence that the payoff is worth the effort.

I know, because I've seen it change countless lives, that the byproducts of double-digit income investing—consistently high monthly income, diversification, protection against volatility, and peace of mind—are well worth the effort involved. I am also supremely confident that the techniques, strategies, and tools that make up this investment style can easily be taught, understood, and put into practice by just about any intelligent, motivated individual out there with enough commitment to themselves.

Next, we are going to walk you through the initial steps necessary to start getting yourself positioned into a double-digit income portfolio. There are a few crucial things you have to do to get your money where it needs to be, so let's get started.

PART FOUR

LET'S GET STARTED BUILDING YOUR OWN 25% CASH MACHINE

16

Five Easy Steps to Getting Started

All the subjects we've covered so far have been designed to get us to this point. You've learned about the new universe of high-yielding income securities and how to evaluate them. You've also seen that generating double-digit income while growing the value of your portfolio comes from the process of actively managing your assets to take advantage of the areas where business conditions are favorable. Finally, you are also now aware that identifying those sectors is a challenge that requires using objective research. Does this sound like a lot of work? Well, it really isn't.

First, consider that the reward for your efforts will be the incredible benefits that double-digit investing can bring, including the peace of mind that comes with knowing your financial needs will be met throughout your retirement years. That should make even the most arduous effort on your part worth the sweat. However, there really is no reason for you to sweat at all.

Part of my job here is to show you how to take the necessary steps when transitioning your assets from a low-yield, low-growth portfolio to a high-yield, high-growth 25% Cash Machine. These steps are easy once you know about them, and with a little guidance, I think you'll find that the path to a fully functioning 25% Cash Machine is much shorter than you ever imagined. Now let's get started.

Step 1—Sell Those Dead-End Dividend Stocks

Remember those dead-end dividend stocks we described in Chapter 4? Well, I have a suspicion that many of you reading this right now have stocks like that stuck in your portfolio. These are equities that are basically dragging down your net worth because of their lackluster performance, and all the while they are paying you a tiny 1 to 3 percent dividend per year—and possibly even a lot less. Some of you probably have stocks in your income portfolio that aren't even paying you any income. If I've "hit the nail on the head" as the cliché goes, then you need to take action, and take action fast.

That's why Step 1 of getting started in the 25% Cash Machine is to sell those dead-end dividend stocks. Think about it for a moment. If your goal is to generate double-digit dividend yields, the first thing you have to do is position your money in the asset classes that actually pay out double-digit returns. Most traditional dividend-paying stocks don't even come close to delivering double-digit income.

So the first item on your to-do list is to call your broker and tell him or her to dump the dead-end dividends. Of course, before you can do this you'll first have to identify these stocks, but I think that's probably a very easy task. Just look for stocks that have lagged behind the rest of the market for some time, and that are paying single-digit dividends. I assure you they won't be too hard to find, because this describes the vast majority of most traditional dividend stocks.

Now in certain cases it may be acceptable to hang on to a traditional dividend-paying stock, particularly if the price of that stock has netted you substantial upside. But the overwhelming majority of traditional dividend stocks aren't going to be huge price performers. They may offer some upside in their share price—certainly more than a money market, CD, or Treasury bond—but definitely not enough for you to hang on to in lieu of a decent-sized dividend yield.

Hey, you can't build a new income portfolio until you dump your underperforming stocks. So the sooner you free yourself from the albatross of low-yielding, dead-end dividend stocks, the sooner you'll be able to start earning those double-digit yields while simultaneously growing the value of your assets.

Step 2—Build a List of Double-Digit Income Securities

Once you've rotated out of those poor-performing, dead-end dividend stocks you'll probably be left holding a lot of cash. And as we've already seen in Chapter 3, we are in a low-income environment, and that means that cash isn't paying much these days. So if you are hanging on to a lot of cash, you won't get very far down the path toward building your own 25% Cash Machine.

Soon after you trim the fat in your income portfolio, you will want to start getting in on the fun that comes from ringing the register each month with those really big dividend payouts. But before you start adding these high-yielding assets to your portfolio, you've got to know which ones they are.

We've already discussed the various asset classes that we use in double-digit income investing (CanRoys, REITs, BDCs, etc.), but here I am not talking about knowing in general terms about the new income assets that funnel you those big returns. I am talking now about knowing the names of specific securities that will give you the best chance at achieving your objectives.

That brings us to the second step you need to take when constructing your own 25% Cash Machine, and that is to start building a list of double-digit income securities. This list should consist of the securities with high yields and low payout ratios. The securities on this list should also have a good track record when it comes to the price performance of the underlying security. It's simply not enough to just look at the dividend yield of a specific security and say that is suitable for inclusion the 25% Cash Machine portfolio.

The securities that make your list have to have some variety, and each category of the new breed of income securities should be represented. It's like a baseball manager with a roster of all-star players. You never know when you will have to take one player out of the game and put another player in, and when that time comes you will want to have your list of all stars ready. Knowing you have a prescreened all-star available will give you the confidence that the player you put in your lineup is going to do the job for you.

There are several ways to start building your list if double-digit income winners, but most require a lot of time, reading and research. The easiest way to start is by looking at Appendix A of this book. Here you'll find a list of the top 100 double-digit income securities that I look at each day in my 25% Cash Machine advisory service.

This list is by no means comprehensive, and depending on when you read this book, some of the securities in this list may have been deleted and replaced with other securities. However, I present this list only as a jumping-off platform for you to see what specific securities we're watching for inclusion in the double-digit income portfolios we manage. If nothing else, it will provide you with a little insight into which securities I think are worth watching.

Step 3—Diversifying Your Income Assets

Step 1 is getting rid of the old, Step 2 is getting a list of income securities together, and that brings us to the next step—a step where we actually start putting securities into our 25% Cash Machine. We will get into the technical aspects of how to properly buy into an income position in the next chapter, but first you've got to realize that a properly functioning 25% Cash Machine thrives on diversity.

Step 3 is diversifying your income assets. Diversification in a high-yield, high-growth portfolio is critical to achieving your performance goals, because diversification of assets helps you guard against a significant downtrend in any given market sector. For a great example of lack of diversification, all you have to do is go back to those Internet boom years. Back then a diversified portfolio consisted of having several different types of Internet stocks. Well, we all saw what happened there, and we never want to let ourselves be exposed to that kind of risk with our income-generating capital.

Through most of 2006, my 25% Cash Machine advisory service was overweight in the energy sector. But just because the fundamentals in this sector were favorable during the year, doesn't mean we didn't also hold a variety of other securities from a wide array of other businesses exhibiting favorable market conditions.

Sure, we could have found enough energy sector securities that met the standards we set for inclusion in the 25% Cash Machine, but why take a chance on being too heavily allocated to energy when there are plenty other sectors with similar potential to provide us with the income and growth we're looking for?

The beauty of diversifying your income assets is that if one of these sectors should happen to break down, we have many others to help our portfolio get us where we need to be. You all know the old adage, "Don't put all your eggs in one basket." Well, it's a perfect way to describe what Step 3 of getting started in double-digit income investing is all about.

Step 4—Become a Student of Dynamic Sector Rotation

We covered the basic tenets of dynamic sector rotation in Chapter 14, and now we get to apply what we've learned in Step 4, becoming a student of dynamic sector rotation. Remember that dynamic sector rotation is just the ability to identify areas of the income-asset world where business and economic conditions are favorable, and of course, where they are unfavorable.

After we've identified the good areas from the bad, we can overweight our portfolio in the sectors with the greatest potential for continued growth, and we can minimize or eliminate our exposure to those areas where conditions are not conducive to achieving our dual goal of 10 percent dividend yields and 15 percent growth.

The most successful income investors try to identify trends before they hit the mainstream; that way they can take positions in securities right before they make their really big moves to the upside. They can also rotate out of, or stay away from certain market sectors where there is bad news on the horizon.

When I say I want you to become a student of sector rotation, it only means that I want you to be aware of the dynamics that influence the various income-generating asset classes we use in the 25% Cash Machine. If you don't know what makes an industry tick, you really aren't going to know when it's time to move in or out of that industry. I guarantee you that learning about what makes markets tick is not only rewarding financially, but it's also just a lot of fun.

Step 5—Decide How You Want to Get Paid

Speaking of fun, now we get to the really fun part of getting started and that is Step 5, deciding how you want to get paid. If you want the income from dividends, distributions, and interest paid out to you each month, the easiest way to do it is by setting up an electronic transfer from your brokerage account to your checking account.

I like to tell my clients to pick a day in the last week of the month to receive their electronic transfer. This way you get most of that month's dividend activity, and you still get your payment in time for the first day of the next month—just in time to cover all of those bills.

Another way to get paid that some people prefer is to basically annualize their projected returns, divide by 12, and then take a fixed amount out each month. This is the more balanced, steady approach because you don't have to speculate or be a slave to a particular month or quarter's dividend activity.

If you're managing your 25% Cash Machine in a tax-deferred account, or if you are in a position where you don't need to actually spend the income you generate, you will likely want to reinvest whichever dividends you can back into more shares of that security. This will compound your earnings, and it will help you achieve the growth in your portfolio that is a key component of double-digit investing.

It is also important that once your 25% Cash Machine portfolio is in place, that you make a schedule of all the ex-dividend and payout dates for each of your holdings. That way you'll know when and how much money is coming into your account in any given month.

I love talking about the different ways to pay yourself and manage your assets. It's a great feeling knowing that one of the steps involved in getting started with double-digit income investing is figuring out when to take a cash disbursement so that you can go out and do the things in life that make it worth living.

Wrap Up

I hope you think that getting started on the primrose path to double-digit returns isn't as difficult as you may have originally thought it would be. All you have to do is follow these five easy steps to getting started, and you'll be that much closer to building that smooth running 25% Cash Machine.

For those of you who want an even easier way to get started with all of this, all you have to do is log on to www.changewave.com. That's the home of Tobin Smith, the ChangeWave Alliance, and it's where you'll find the 25% Cash Machine advisory service.

It's your one-stop shop for all things double-digit investing. Here's where you'll find the current 25% Cash Machine portfolio recommendations. In addition to the latest picks, I provide a weekly commentary on the markets, as well as a monthly newsletter that profiles a different income-asset class each month. Each month's newsletter is also replete with lots of news and helpful hints on how to maximize your results in your very own 25% Cash Machine.

17

Crafting a Double-Digit Income Portfolio

In the preceding chapter, we went over the five steps to take when you first get started with double-digit investing. Once you've become familiar with these steps and once you've incorporated them into your own income investing platform, you will need to start considering some of the finer points associated with our strategy.

In this chapter, we are going to take a look at a look at a few of these finer points, and we'll explain some of the subtleties that go along crafting a double-digit income portfolio. The following is a series of helpful hints, and explanatory notes of some of the intricacies and nuances of a double-digit portfolio. Getting acquainted with these finer points should help fill in any gaps you may have in your understanding of how a 25% Cash Machine operates.

Afterward, we'll give you a peek at some of the cornerstone security selections in the 25% Cash Machine advisory service portfolio. Reading about some of our actual selections will help you understand what goes in to our investment decisions. And, understanding why and how we do it the way we do can help you do it right for yourself.

Realistic Expectations

The first thing you need to realize about this strategy is that it is not meant to be a trading account. You will not be looking to book short-term gains in 30, 60, or 90 days after you enter a position. That's not what the 25% Cash Machine is about. What you should be looking to do is hold each and every position you have for years to come.

If you do your homework, buy into the right securities with the right fundamentals in the right industries, the results will be high-dividend yields and consistent, steady price appreciation. Now, with that said, you also must have realistic expectations concerning the performance of double-digit income securities.

You cannot and should not expect these securities to trade like pure growth stocks. Sure, they will move up to some degree on favorable news, but not like common stocks that retain all their earnings and pay out zero dividends. Double-digit income securities should not be used in a portfolio whose principal goal is generating short-term gains. These securities should be used for what for what they were designed to do, which is to generate high yields and deliver consistent annual growth.

Know Your Objectives

I want you to keep in mind that the reason you are building this 25% Cash Machine is so you can generate a 10 percent annual income stream while also pursuing an additional 15 percent capital appreciation over time.

Always remember that this is your income portfolio, a portfolio that you are going to build and keep for the rest of your life. You will likely not get a 25 percent total return every year on your money with double-digit investing. Some years you may get more, and some years you may get less, but over time this approach is designed to generate that 25 percent average total return.

Keeping this objective at the forefront of your decision-making process will help you stay focused on the task at hand, and it will keep you from getting distracted by other so-called investment "opportunities" that don't fit into your plan. Be ruthless in your quest for double-digit income and 15 percent growth. If it doesn't fit the plan, it isn't worth your time or money.

A Highly Focused Portfolio

You aren't in the mutual fund business. You don't have to buy 200 different positions to ensure you have the proper level of diversification in your portfolio. Sure, you do have to diversify your assets to guard against a big drop in any one market sector, but when you are crafting your double-digit income portfolio you want to have a portfolio of about 20 to 25 securities. I say if you have more than 25, you probably have too many.

Taking a Full 4 percent Position

I thought it would be constructive to go over what I mean when I say "take a full 4 percent position" regarding specific recommendations. From my keyboard, it's easy to get swayed into thinking everyone is on board with how to build your own strategic high-income portfolio, assuming that you have read all of this book leading up to your decision to get involved. However, that isn't always the case.

That said, let's lay out just what a full 4 percent position is and why it's important. First, it is my intention for you to own at least 25 stocks in your double-digit income portfolio. (For another example, we could own 50 stocks at 2 percent, and so on.) In doing so, we can apply a little math here to determine how much of each stock you should own so as to equally weight your holdings. It's pretty simple. Say you take $100,000 and divide it by 25 holdings. You come up with the 4 percent figure I'm talking about, meaning you would put roughly $4,000 in each recommendation.

This 4 percent figure seems to be a happy medium between diversification and risk/reward ratio. What I mean by that is I don't want you to be overweighted in any one stock because if that stock were to implode, it wouldn't rock the overall portfolio too much. However, if the stock were to take off to the upside, I want to know that its gain would be material to the overall performance numbers from year to year.

From a fund manager's perspective, there are few things more frustrating than owning too little of the few stocks that can make your year. A giant mutual fund that has only half of 1 percent in Google shares last year doesn't move the needle that much if the fund has equal amounts of laggards like Microsoft, Dell, Intel, and eBay.

If I'm running a high-beta portfolio full of biotech and nanotechnology companies, I'm going to want to really spread my risk to say 100 to 200 stocks simply because of the high P/E ratios and untested fundamentals. But a low-risk portfolio allows me to shorten my holdings list to 20 to 30 names so as to get more bang for my buck. That's how it works when it comes to running other people's dough and it is a good rule to follow when it comes to running your own dough.

I believe in having some concentration within your portfolio, but this doesn't mean having only a few equity holdings. In fact, in order to manage the potential downside in any one security, I don't like to have any single position that is over 5 percent of my total portfolio.

I think a 5 percent position in any one security is actually the ideal amount, because it is large enough for a stock that is working well to have plenty of impact on the overall portfolio, but small enough so that if a position goes against me, it doesn't blow up the total return for the whole year. This 5 percent game is one of the subtle aspects to the principle of diversification, which as we saw in Chapter 16 plays a key role in a properly functioning 25% Cash Machine.

Pick Your Spots

Most of the securities you'll be buying and holding in your 25% Cash Machine portfolio can be considered stocks. Yes, they are stocks with serious yields and they don't fit the traditional definition of a stock, but nevertheless they are considered stocks.

Any professional stock trader will jokingly tell you that a good trade bought incorrectly just becomes an investment. And even though you are not treating your income portfolio as you would a short-term trading account where the exact price execution point is paramount, it is helpful to learn how to buy securities correctly. Part of learning how to buy securities correctly is learning to avoid chasing them on their way up.

Most of the securities you'll be buying in your own 25% Cash Machine will be priced under $40 per share, and therefore a couple points can mean a big difference in your total return. If you can time your entry points correctly, you'll be that much closer to reaching your performance goals.

Incremental Purchases

If a security is trading at a higher level than I really want to pay, sometimes I'll buy into it in thirds, meaning I will buy one-third of it now, one-third if it dips, and another third if it keeps going up. Often getting a good price on a dividend security is a matter of timing.

You will usually have to purchase these securities right after they have paid a dividend to get them at a discount price. Sure, you'll have to wait another month or even a quarter for your next dividend payment, but your long-term cost basis has been established at what is probably going to be your best near-term level.

The Rule of 72

Do you know the Rule of 72? It's just a little device investment professionals use to demonstrate the speed with which your money can grow. Basically what you do is take the number 72 and divide it by the return you're getting on your money. This formula tells you how many years it will take for you to double your money.

For example, if you're making 10 percent per year on your money, it will take you 7.2 years to double your current principal. Not bad, but now let's put in the numbers we're looking to get through double-digit investing. If you are making 25 percent on your money, it will only take you 2.88 years to double it. Now that's really good, and it's what this whole book and my advisory service is all about.

A Dose of Reality

Well, so much for the finer points, subtleties, and tips of crafting a 25% Cash Machine portfolio. Now I am sure you'd like to see some real-world examples of those high-income securities that we've actually purchased in a real 25% Cash Machine advisory service. Up until now it's been mostly theory. Now it's time for a dose of reality.

The following two securities represent some of the very first ones chosen when we initially began building our very own 25% Cash Machine. The process we used to select these securities was the very same one I've outlined for you in the preceding pages.

We selected from many of the new income-securities available today that weren't around even 10 years ago. We analyzed their payout ratios to make sure they were low enough to help the company keep growing, and we used our ChangeWave Alliance research to help us determine the favorability of the market conditions that most influence these particular sectors. It's time now to call out their names, along with some of the reasoning behind why we like each of these double-digit income securities.

Primewest Energy

PrimeWest Energy Trust is an open-ended investment trust which engages in the acquisition, development, production, and sale of natural gas, crude oil, and natural gas liquids. It primarily focuses its business on the western Canadian sedimentary basin. The trust was formed under the laws of Alberta in 1996 and is headquartered in Calgary, Canada.

Back in March 2005, the brokerage firm and investment bank Lehman Brothers upgraded PrimeWest Energy Trust to "equal-weight" from "underweight" based on valuation. The broker told its clients that its acquisition of western Canadian assets from Calpine Energy had afforded the trust the ability to raise its monthly distribution two times this year while still maintaining a conservative payout ratio of 74 to 76 percent. Apparently, Lehman's analysis was spot on.

On August 2 of that year, PrimeWest reported distributions in the second quarter 2005 were $0.90 per unit, which represented a payout ratio of approximately 70 percent of operating cash flow. That's a really attractive payout ratio, and it's one of the chief reasons we chose PrimeWest in our own portfolio.

American Capital Strategies

Another one of our initial 25% Cash Machine holdings is business development company American Capital Strategies. This hybrid financial lender was extremely well positioned within its respective industry evidenced by its very strong five-year track record at the time of our initial purchase.

Just about every week there is news of yet another major merger or takeover of some sort. The pace of mergers and acquisitions (M&A) has picked up dramatically in recent years, but most people only hear about the big deals that make the financial press. In addition to the multibillion dollar deals are literally hundreds of buyouts occurring in all manner of industries.

The great thing about BDCs is that now income investors can buy a professionally managed pool of money that is heavy into this market, affording us the ability to profit well from the abundance of M&A activity.

American Capital Strategies is one of those publicly traded buyout and mezzanine funds that you just can't ignore when crafting a double-digit income portfolio. The company has capital resources exceeding $5.2 billion, and its business is diversified. It has three main lines of business: a financial partner in management and employee buyouts; a provider of senior debt, mezzanine, and equity financing for buyouts led by private equity firms; and a provider of capital directly to private and small public companies.

This BDC generally invests up to $150 million in each transaction and, since its August 1997 initial public offering (IPO), has invested approximately $5 billion in nearly 150 portfolio companies. Its portfolio companies include services, transportation, construction, wholesale, retail, healthcare, and industrial, consumer, chemical, and food products. That's a lot of diversification within its own industry; those numbers don't lie. They demonstrate to me that this company is a well-managed industry, with a lot of room to grow.

Putting It All Together

I know I have merely scratched the surface in telling you about just two of the companies we selected for inclusion in our 25% Cash Machine advisory service portfolio. And while I am pretty confident many of you are screaming for more detail on the complete contents of this portfolio, the changing nature of our holdings precludes us from presenting them here in this forum. For a complete list of equities in the 25% Cash Machine advisory service, you'll need to go to our web site at ChangeWave.com.

Well, there you have it. We've covered all of the basic theory and most of the "how to" involved in getting yourself on the right track toward generating double-digit returns while enhancing the value of your income-generating assets.

The way I see it, with the cost of goods and services rising on the things we need most, and with the pittance that traditional income securities have handed us over the years, there really is no other choice than to take action and do something different. I think double-digit investing is the answer to all of the issues I've raised, but I don't expect you to just take it from me.

I do, however, expect any thinking individual to take away from this book the basic knowledge that there is a better way to manage income assets, and that you don't have to settle for mediocrity when it comes to funding the rest of your life.

Constructing Your Double-Digit Income Portfolio

It's one thing to have all the information you need. It's quite another to know how to put it to work. In this section, I want to provide a game plan for constructing a double-digit portfolio. The good news is that I designed this strategy so that income investors could set this program up with relative ease. So here we go. Follow these steps and you'll be up and running in your high-yield account in no time.

First, open an online brokerage account. If you don't have one already, consider any of the big names like TDAmeritrade, Fidelity, or E-Trade. I'm not partial to Schwab because you might wait an hour to get some assis-

tance running a trade or fixing a problem. No one talks to Chuck. Chuck puts you on perma-hold and hopes you'll hang up out of pure frustration. That firm is the house of pain for retail customers.

If you are using a full-service broker, sign up for the same features and negotiate a discount on unsolicited trades. Those are trades where you call your broker and tell him or her what and how much to buy. A discount is appropriate since you are calling the shots and the broker is simply taking an order to fill a trade.

The next thing you need to do is fund the account, typically by check or wire transfer from your bank to the brokerage firm. Once those funds have cleared, you are ready to begin buying some securities. To take full advantage of the 25% Cash Machine strategy, you'll want to have enough capital to buy at least 10 positions in which invest in. So you're going to need at least $25,000 to $50,000 to get going, and preferably $100,000 and higher so as to make this program cost efficient.

Think about it. If you only have $25,000 to invest and you want to buy all 25 current recommendations on the ChangeWave Buy List, then you end up putting $1,000 in 25 stocks. At a cost of $11 per trade, you are going to spend $275.00, or 1.1 percent, of your capital just to position the account. That same $275 cost for running 25 trades in a $100,000 account amounts to only 0.00275 percent or roughly three-tenths of 1 percent.

With most online brokerages, you can develop watch lists and follow news to some extent, but for the most part, these web sites are limited in how much information and news is generated as well as having the capacity to monitor your portfolio. For this reason, I use Briefing.com as a news service and DTNIQ as a streaming service for monitoring several watch lists.

I'm a professional asset manager, so I need these tools, but if you're managing your own money and have an account in excess of $100,000 in value, I would highly suggest spending the extra $100 per month for having these services at your fingertips. A powerful news platform keeps you posted on the day's events, economic data, earnings dates, earnings guidance, conference schedules, stock splits, market commentary, sector strength, technical indicators, broker upgrades/downgrades, IPOs, and merger activity.

If you are serious about your money, trying to stay up with the market by watching CNBC or clicking on to the New York Times *web site or the*

Drudge Report is not going to cut it. I highly recommend a market-focused news service to keep you up to speed on what's happening all the time in markets here in the United States and overseas.

Using a streaming service like DTNIQ affords me the ability to follow literally hundreds of stocks. I break them out sector by sector on different lists and on different screens. My watch lists for high-yield securities is about 300 names deep and I segregate it by sector: CanRoys, MLPs, shipping/tanker stocks, closed-end funds, brick-and-mortar REITs, mortgage REITs, BDCs, commodity trusts, foreign securities, preferred stocks, IDSs, CBTs, and others.

In setting up my dynamic watch lists this way, I can see the daily money flow moving in and out of various sectors, which helps me determine whether I'm in the right areas of the economy and whether I need to investigate any sector-wide developments. I may want to increase or decrease my exposure relative to how a sector is behaving and seeing it all trade in relation to each other really helps me know whether fund managers, or the "smart money," agrees with what I'm doing or not. And we do want to know what the smart money is doing. Fund buying can be the wind at your back—or the spray in your face.

The last and most important step to setting up your strategic high-income system is to subscribe to a professional online high yield advisory service, preferably mine, The ChangeWave 25% Cash Machine. I do the stock picking, you run the trades. Like any sport, having a great coach will take you to levels of performance that would be difficult to achieve on your own. A good online advisory service will train you and show you how to use the tools you have to the best of your ability. That's what great coaches do and is fully what my objective is with our approach. Give a man a fish and you've fed him for a day; teach him to fish and you've fed him for life. There's great truth in that statement.

This strategy, properly understood and implemented, is timeless. You can pass on this knowledge to your spouse, your children, your grandchildren, your friends, and associates. This is the real beauty of the program, it's not hard to grasp and it works, year after year after year.

Once you have established your lists and logged on to your news service, you are ready to begin building your account. At this juncture, instead of going hog wild and buying every name on the buy list, I would choose the top 10 or so "fresh money" buys that a good advisory service offers. This gives you a solid foundation to construct the balance of the portfolio, exercising patience to establish good entry points. Timing matters and matters a lot. Don't dive right in, pick your spots and buy stocks on down market days.

After you have placed your first 10 names in your portfolio, add accordingly and fill out the balance of your account with the rest of the recommended buy-rated securities. From there, keep an eye on your portfolio, learn along the way by observing, and listen to the advice of your high-yield adviser until you have gained the knowledge and experience to do this on your own. And even at that point, you want to know what the high-yield community is saying, all the time, about what you own and don't own. Remember, this is not a static portfolio. It takes constant monitoring and a willingness to move when necessary. Once you get a handle on this process, you'll truly be in control of your income. I promise.

18

A New Level of Confidence

Throughout this book, I've laid out a primer on what I believe to be the best way to generate a solid stream of dividends on your money each month while also allowing that money to grow. I fully believe that by following the tenets and principles of double-digit investing, and by constructing your own 25% Cash Machine you'll be prepared to meet most financial challenges you will ever face head on, and with the utmost confidence.

And let's face it; isn't having enough money really about being able to confront your needs with confidence? The confidence of knowing that no matter what happens, you are going to be okay? Think about the calm and peace of mind you'll enjoy from not having to worry about making ends meet. Imagine yourself independently wealthy, with a steady stream of income taking care of all your needs and desires for the rest of your life.

I am here to tell you that this level of confidence is indeed possible. How do I know? Because over the years, thousands of my clients, as well as the thousands who've joined my 25% Cash Machine advisory service, are living proof of the power and efficacy of double-digit investing.

Everyday people just like you are using the income they've received from one of the new breed of high-yield securities out there to help make their lives better, more interesting, and more meaningful. They are using this income to help themselves, their families, their friends, and their communities function better.

The high double-digit yields these investors are achieving enable them to enjoy the freedom that comes from not worrying about ever having to go back into the workforce after they retire. This enhanced income is also allowing them to pay for things like a college education for their children and grandchildren, and for helping loved ones with unexpected medical expenses.

Some are now even able to pay for those little extras such as that exotic sports car they've always dreamed of owning. I know that it may sound frivolous to aspire to own some six-figure automobile, but the point here is that no matter what your income needs or desires, double-digit investing can help you fulfill your ambitions.

One of the things I'm most proud of is what my system is able to do for people with special needs, such as my friend Caren who you read about in the Introduction. Her ability to generate enough income after the tragic loss of her husband so that she was able to stay home and take care of her autistic child is just one of a plethora of success stories that can be attributed to double-digit investing.

I don't like to be boastful, but I can honestly say that having been in the investment field for nearly 25 years, there is simply no other method out there that I am aware of that can help you meet your income needs the way a properly functioning 25% Cash Machine can. The proof is in the pudding as the cliché reads, and in this case, the pudding is investors out there like my friend Caren.

The Rest Is Up to You

My goal with this book has been to expose you all to a new way of thinking about dividend paying securities in general, and specifically the strategies I've developed to best harness the power of these new securities.

If you're an investor who's been frustrated with your results on the income front, I urge you to take the action I've outlined in this book and get yourself started on the road to a new level of confidence. Before long, you'll be in the same position as those thousands of other investors who have already built their own 25% Cash Machine and who are ringing that register each and every month.

As I've done throughout these pages, I can tell you all about the details of the new breed of high-yielding securities. I can also tell you how to use them. I can even tell you how to get started and what steps to take to get yourself on track to building your wealth through double-digit investing. There is one thing, however, that I cannot do for you. That one thing is something we all must do for ourselves, and in this respect, we are all alone.

This one thing that I am speaking of requires a simple act of volition, an exercising of your own will on behalf your best interest. Simply put, it means making the choice for a better way of life—a better way of life that comes from the security and peace of mind that a high level of income can bring. It means making the choice to get started building your own 25% Cash Machine.

It may sound simple, even self-evident, but one of the biggest obstacles keeping people from achieving what they want in life is fear. Fear of the unknown, fear of loss, fear of making a mistake, even fear of success. I understand this fear all too well. We all have to overcome the barriers and climb over the walls we've constructed for ourselves. As humans, it's natural for us to be fearful of a negative outcome and to try to avoid it.

So, rather than discard that fear entirely, focus on the fear you are going to feel without the confidence of knowing that you and your family will be taken care of financially no matter what the circumstances. Think about having to live through your retirement years dependent on family or the state. This is the kind of fear can be a real motivator, and it's a kind of healthy fear that can compel even the most risk-averse among us to take action toward a better outcome.

Parting Thoughts

If you take nothing else away from this book, please know that there is a better way to achieve your financial goals. You don't have to be restricted to mediocrity when it comes to making your money work for you. The powers that be on Wall Street want you to think what they are handing you is high income, but all it really is is a lazy way to peddle you securities.

If you are currently struggling with ways to make your money work for you, double-digit income investing the 25% Cash Machine way is your white knight. In the span of just a couple of months, you can really rev up your income using a proven strategy that delivers high monthly dividend payouts while also putting your money in a position to keep growing. And as that principal grows, you'll continue getting bigger and bigger monthly dividends. In my opinion, it just doesn't get any better than that.

It is my hope that everyone who reads this primer on double-digit income investing finds the information and advice useful and applicable to their very own situation. I also hope that if you've found this book enlightening, helpful, or just an interesting read that you recommend it to a friend or colleague who you think may benefit from its contents. Helping out others is one of the most rewarding things we can do in life, so if you know someone who could use a little help with his or her financial future, why not buy them their own copy of *The 25% Cash Machine*?

My final and perhaps greatest hope is that now, after having read all about double-digit investing, you are filled with a tremendous sense of possibility: a sense that you don't have to settle for conventional returns, a conventional retirement, or even a conventional life.

Money is by no means the key to happiness, but not having to worry about money is something that will improve all our lives. It is my wish that by creating your own 25% Cash Machine your life will improve greatly. If I have helped you to do that, then I will have helped the world become a better place for us all.

APPENDIX A

SECTORS AND INVESTMENTS

Business Development Companies (BDCs)

American Capital Securities (ACAS)
Apollo Investment (AINV)
Allied Capital (ALD)
Ares Capital (ARCC)
Gramercy Capital (GKK)
iStar Financial (SFI)
Prospect Energy Corp. (PSEC)
RAIT Investment Trust (RAS)

Canadian Business Trusts

Arctic Glacier Income Fund (AGUNF)
Precision Drilling Trust (PDS)
Primary Energy Recycling (PYGYF)
VersaCold Income Fund (VCLDF)

Canadian Energy Trusts

Canetic Resources Trust (CNE)
Enerplus Resources Fund (ERF)

Harvest Energy Trust (HTE)
Penn West Energy Trust (PWE)
PrimeWest Energy (PWI)
Pengrowth Energy Trust (PGH)
Provident Energy Trust (PVX)

Closed-End Funds

Aberdeen Australia Equity Fund (IAF)
Alliance National Municipal Income Fund (AFB)
Blackrock Preferred Opportunity Trust (BPP)
Blue Chip Value Fund (BLU)
Chartwell Dividend & Income Fund (CWF)
Credit Suisse Asset Management Income (CIK)
Gabelli Utility Trust (GUT)
H&Q Healthcare Investors (HQH)
ING Global Equity Dividend & Premium Fund (IGD)
Munivest Fund (MFV)
Nuveen Municipal High Income Opportunities Fund (NMZ)
Pioneer High Income Trust (PHT)
Prospect Street High Income (PHY)
RMR Real Estate Fund (RMR)
Salomon Brothers Emerging Market Debt Fund (ESD)
Zweig Fund (ZF)

Convertible Securities

Advent/Claymore Enhanced Growth & Income (LCM)
Calamos Convertible Opportunities & Income Fund (CHI)
Lord Abbett Bond-Debenture Fund (LBNDX)
Nicholas Applegate Convertible & Income Fund (NCV)
Franklin Investment Convertible (FISCX)
Davis Appreciation & Income (RPFCX)

Corporate Bonds

Blackrock High Yield Trust (BHY)
Corporate High Yield Fund (HYV)
Credit Suisse High Yield Bond Fund (DHY)

New American High Yield Fund (HYB)
PIMCO Corporate Opportunity Fund (PTY)
Scudder High Income Trust (KHI)

Income Deposit Securities (IDSs) or Enhanced Income Securities (EISs)

B&G Foods (BGF)
Centerplate (CVP)
Coinmach Service (DRY)
Otelco Inc. (OTT)
Xerium Technology (XRM)

Master Limited Partnerships (MLPs)

Alliance Resource Partners (ARLP)
AmeriGas Partners, LP (APU)
Buckeye Partners LP (BPL)
Calumet Specialty Products Partners LP (CLMT)
Capono Energy LLC (CPNO)
Crosstex Energy LP (XTEX)
Dorchester Minerals, LP (DMLP)
Enbridge Energy Partners, LP (EEP)
Energy Transfer Partners (ETP)
Ferrellgas Partners LP (FGP)
Highland Partners LP (HLND)
Kinder Morgan Energy Partners (KMP)
Oneok Partners LP (OKS)
Plains All-America Pipeline (PAA)
Suburban Propane Partners LP (SPH)
Sunoco Logistics Partners LP (SXL)
Terra Nitrogen LP (TNH)
Transmontaigne Partners LP (TLP)
Valero LP (VLI)

Oil/Shipping/Tanker Stocks

Aries Maritime Transport Ltd. (RAMS)
Arlington Tankers Ltd. (ATB)
Diana Shipping (DSX)

Double Hull Tankers (DHT)
Dryships Inc. (DRYS)
Eagle Bulk Shipping (EGLE)
Frontline, Ltd. (FRO)
Genco Shipping & Trading (GSTL)
General Maritime (GMR)
Knightsbridge Tankers (VLCCF)
Nordic American Tanker Shipping (NAT)
Quintana Maritime Ltd. (QMAR)
Tsakos Energy (TNP)

Real Estate Investment Trusts (REITs)

Commercial Net Leasing Realty Investment (CNL)
Crescent Real Estate Equity (CEI)
Glimcher Realty (GRT)
Health Care REIT (HCN)
Hospitality Properties (HPT)
HRPT Properties (HRP)
Impac Mortgage Holdings (IMH)
Long Term Care Properties (LTC)
Medical Properties Trust (MPW)
MFA Mortgage Investments (MFA)
MGC Capital Corp. (MCGC)
Nationwide Health Properties (NHP)
New Century Financial (NEW)
Novastar Financial (NFI)
Realty Income (O)
Senior Housing Properties (SNH)
Tanger Factory Outlet Centers (SKT)
Thornburg Mortgage (TMA)
Universal Health Realty (UHT)
Windrose Medical Properties (WRS)

APPENDIX B

RESOURCES

Sector Associations

Canada's Office of Consumer Affairs & Industry for Canada
235 Queen Street, 6th Floor
Ottawa, Ontario K1A 0H5
Telephone: (613) 946-2576
Fax: (613) 952-6927
E-mail: consumer.information@ic.gc.ca

Closed End Fund Association (CEFA), Inc.
P.O. Box 28037
Kansas City, MO 64188
Telephone: (816) 413-8900
E-mail: CEFA@CEFA.com

INTERTANKO North America (Shipping Tankers)
801 North Quincy Street
Suite 200
Arlington, VA 22203
Telephone: (703) 373-2269
Fax: (703) 841-0389
E-mail: washington@intertanko.com

National Association of Home Builders (NAHB)
1201 15th Street, NW
Washington, DC 20005
Telephone: (202) 266-8200
       (800) 368-5242
Fax: (202) 266-8400

National Association of Real Estate Investment Trusts (NAREIT)
1875 I Street, NW
Suite 600
Washington DC 20006
Telephone: (202) 739-9400
       (800) 3-NAREIT
E-mail: info@nareit.com

National Mining Association
101 Constitution Avenue, NW
Suite 500 East
Washington, DC 20001-2133
Telephone: (202) 463-2600
Fax: (202) 463-2666
www.nma.org

Publicly Traded Partnerships (Master Limited Partnerships)
1801 K Street, NW
Suite 500
Washington, DC 20006
Telephone: (202) 973-3150
Fax: (202) 973-3101

Online Resources

Bankrate.com
11760 US HWY 1
Suite 500
North Palm Beach, FL 33408
Telephone: (561) 630-2400
Fax: (561) 625-4540

Bigcharts.com
MarketWatch, Inc.
201 California St.
San Francisco, CA 94111

Briefing.com
Telephone: (800) 752-3013
E-mail: service@briefing.com

The 25% Cash Machine Newsletter
ChangeWave Research
2420A Gehman Lane
Lancaster, PA 17602
Telephone: (888) 225-9373
E-mail: service@changewave.com

Data Transmission Network (DTN)
9110 West Dodge Road
Suite 200
Omaha, NE 68114
Telephone: (800) 475-4755
www.dtniq.com

Investor's Business Daily
Telephone: (800) 831-2525
www.investors.com

RiskMetrics Group
One Chase Manhattan Plaza
44th Floor
New York, NY 10005
Telephone: (212) 981-7475
www.riskgrades.com

U.S. Department of Agriculture
1400 Independence Avenue, SW
Washington, DC 20250
www.usda.com

U.S. Department of Energy (DOE)
1000 Independence Avenue, SW
Washington, DC 20585
Telephone: (202) 586-5000
www.energy.gov

U.S. Department of Commerce
1401 Constitution Avenue, NW
Washington, DC 20230
www.commerce.gov

U.S. Department of Labor Statistics
Postal Square Building
2 Massachusetts Avenue, NE
Washington, DC 20212-0001
Telephone: (202) 691-5200
Fax: (202) 691-6325
www.bls.com

Wall Street Journal Online
200 Liberty Street
New York, NY 10281
Telephone: (212) 416-2000
www.wsj.com

YahooFinance.com
Yahoo! Inc.
701 First Avenue
Sunnyvale, CA 94089
Telephone: (408) 349-3300

APPENDIX C

GLOSSARY

Accumulated Dividend: Dividend due to stockholders of cumulative preferred stock that has not been paid to them. Until the dividend is paid, it is carried on the corporation's books as a liability.

Adjusted Basis: The base price that is used to assess capital gains and losses when a security is sold. When net proceeds are used for tax purposes, the commissions are deducted at the time of sale. If any stock splits have occurred since the original purchase, the stock's price needs to be adjusted to obtain a correct adjusted basis.

American Depository Receipt (ADR): Receipt for shares of a foreign-based corporation held by a U.S. banking institution. ADRs are created to facilitate transactions and transfers of ownership of foreign securities in the United States.

Appreciation: Appreciation is an asset's increase in value.

Asset Allocation: The allotment of investment funds amongst various types of assets such as cash equivalents, stock, fixed-income investments, real estate, and precious metals. It also applies to subclassifications such as industry groupings of common stocks and government, municipal, and corporate bonds. Asset allocation affects both risk and return.

Asset-Backed Securities: Securities underwritten by brokerage firms who sell them to investors. The securities (bonds or notes) are backed by loan paper or accounts receivable of the issuer.

Baby Boomer: A baby boomer is someone born in a period of increased birth rates, such as those during the economic prosperity following World War II. In the United States, demographers have put the generation's birth years at 1946 to 1964, though the U.S. birth rate (per 1,000 population) actually began to decline after 1957.

Business Development Company (BDC): A vehicle established by Congress to allow smaller, retail investors to participate in and benefit from investing in small private businesses as well as the revitalization of larger private companies.

Canadian Royalty Trusts: A royalty trust is a type of corporation usually involved in mining. It is taxed according to special regulations, whereby its profits are not taxed at the corporate level provided a certain high percentage (e.g., 90 percent) of profits are distributed to share holders as dividends. The dividends are then taxed as personal income. This system, similar to Real Estate Investment Trusts, effectively avoids the double taxation of corporate dividends.

Capital Gains: The positive difference between an asset's purchase price and the selling price. Current tax regulations require any gains to be taxed at a rate up to 39.6 percent.

Capital Gains Distribution: A distribution of profits derived from the assets within a mutual fund. Mutual funds usually distribute these gains on a quarterly basis to their shareholders. These gains are currently taxable at a rate up to 28 percent.

Cash Dividend: A cash payment that is made to shareholders of corporate stock. The dividends are distributed from current earnings or accumulated profits. Current tax regulations require cash dividends to be taxed as income.

Closed-End Fund: An investment company that issues a fixed number of shares and is usually listed on a stock exchange. An investor who wishes to buy shares must purchase them from investors who wish to sell their shares. They do not deal with the investment company directly.

Convertible Preferred Stock: A preferred stock that may be exchanged into common shares at the owner's option as long as it is in accordance with the issue's terms.

Convertible Securities: Corporate securities (usually preferred stock or bonds) that are exchangeable into a fixed number of shares of common stock at a stipulated price. Convertibles may also be exchanged into other forms of the security, but it is unusual. Convertible securities are usually bought by investors who want higher income than what can be received from common stock combined with a greater potential for appreciation than what can be received from regular bonds. A corporation will issue convertibles to enhance the marketability of their securities.

Corporate Bond: Debt instrument issued by a corporation. In contrast to most municipal and government bonds, which are not traded on major exchanges and are tax free, corporate bonds are traded on major exchanges and the interest paid to the investor is taxable.

Cost Basis: The original cost of security. When the security is sold, the difference between the sale price and basis is the income or loss reported at that time on U.S. tax returns.

Current Yield: The current yield refers only to the yield of a bond or stock at the current moment. It is the annual interest rate paid by a bond or stock, expressed as a percentage of its current market price.

Declaration Date: A specified date that the board of directors of a corporation declares and authorizes a dividend payment. At this time, the dividend becomes a corporate obligation.

Diversification: Spreading risk by placing assets in different types of investments (i.e., mutual funds, stocks, bonds) and various companies in different industry groups (i.e., pharmaceutical, utility, airline).

Dividend: Distribution of a company's earnings to its shareholders, usually in the form of a quarterly check. The company's board of directors authorize and determine the amount of the dividend. Dividends are taxed as income in the year they are received by the shareholder. A mutual fund dividend is paid out of income and the shareholder's tax is dependent on whether the distributions originated from interest income, capital gains, or dividends received by the fund.

Dividend Frequency: The frequency in which a dividend pays (i.e., monthly, quarterly, semi-annually).

Dividend Payout Ratio: Percentage of earnings paid in cash to shareholders. It is calculated by dividing the dividends paid on common stock by the earnings per share. In general, a corporation with a higher payout ratio will be more mature. A company in a growth phase usually reinvests all earnings and pays little or no dividends.

Dividend Reinvestment Plan (DRIP): A program in which a dividend paying company (especially mutual funds) will automatically reinvest an investor's dividend to purchase additional shares of the company's stock. The dividend is still taxable by the IRS. In participating in a DRIP, investors use dollar-cost averaging to increase their amount of capital in the stock.

Dividends Payable: Dollar amount of dividends that are obligated to be paid once a dividend is declared by the board of directors. The dollar amount is listed as a liability in the annual and quarterly reports.

Dividend Yield: The annual percentage of return that the dividend provides to the investor on either common or preferred stock—often referred to as just "yield." The yield is calculated by dividing the annual cash dividend per share by the stock's market price at the time of purchase.

Emerging Market Debt: A term used to encompass bonds issued by less developed countries. It does not include borrowing from government, supranational organizations such as the IMF or private sources, though loans that are securitized and issued to the markets would be included.

Exchange Traded Fund (ETF): Open-ended collective investment schemes, traded as shares on most global stock exchanges. Typically, ETFs try to replicate a stock market index such as the S&P 500 or Hang Seng Index, a market sector such as energy or technology, or a commodity such as gold or petroleum.

Ex-Dividend Date: A synonym for "without dividend," it is the time period between a dividend announcement and payment during which an investor who buys the stock's shares is not entitled to receive the dividend. For example, a dividend may be declared as payable to holders of record on the company's books on a given Friday (the record date). The New York Stock Exchange would declare the stock "ex-dividend" as of the opening of the market on the preceding Wednesday (two business days prior to the record date). Therefore, an investor who buys the stock on or after that Wednesday is not entitled to that dividend. It is common for a stock's price to increase by the dividend amount as the ex-dividend date gets closer. It then usually drops by the dividend amount after the ex-dividend date. A stock that is ex-dividend is marked with an "x" in the stock table listings in newspapers.

Grantor Trust: A trust in which the grantor retains some interests and control and therefore is taxed on any income from the trust.

Hybrid Financial Lending: I use the term "hybrid" to describe the sector of the market that is primarily engaged in the business of what is called "bridge financing" or "mezzanine financing." What this simply means is that they lend to various entities, not bound by a specific proxy statement. They get involved in financing mergers and acquisitions, leveraged buyouts (LBOs), lending to small- to medium-sized businesses, speculative commercial construction and various other non-traditional entities like venture capital.

Income Deposit Securities (IDSs): IDSs are a new type of security debuting in the United States on the Amex. While new issues will vary, the following features and benefits will generally be applicable to all IDSs: Designed to pay monthly income, IDSs are designed to pay a monthly income stream based on interest payments on the notes and dividend income, if any, on the common stock.

Income Stock: A stock with a history of paying consistently high dividends.

Inflation: The persistent and appreciable rise in the prices of goods and services. Moderate inflation is normally associated with periods of expansion and high employment—increasing dollars chasing a dwindling supply of goods. Hyperinflation, when prices rise 100 percent or more a year, causes people to lose confidence in the currency. During inflationary times, people often divert their investments into real estate and gold because they usually retain their value.

Inflation Rate: Rate of price changes usually calculated on a monthly or annual basis. The Consumer Price Index and the Producer Price

Index are two principle U.S. indicators of inflation rates. They track changes in prices paid by consumers and producers.

Initial Public Offering (IPO): The first sale of a corporation's common shares to public investors. The main purpose of an IPO is to raise capital for the corporation. The term refers only to the first public issuance of a company's shares; any later public issuance of shares is referred to as a Secondary Market Offering.

Limited Liability Company (LLC): A type of company, authorized only in certain states, whose owners and managers receive the limited liability and (usually) tax benefits of an S Corporation without having to conform to the S corporation restrictions.

Master Limited Partnership (MLP): Investment that combines the tax benefits of a limited partnership with the liquidity of publicly traded securities.

Mortgage-Backed Securities: Securities backed by a pool of mortgages, such as those issued by Ginnie Mae and Freddie Mac, also called mortgage-backed certificates.

Option Income Fund: A mutual fund that attempts to increase current income through continual option writing.

Ordinary Income: Income other than capital gains.

Payment Date: The date on which a dividend, mutual fund distribution, or bond interest payment is made or scheduled to be made; also called distribution date.

Preferred Stocks: A preferred stock is a type of capital stock that pays dividends at a set rate (at the time of issuance). Dividend payments to preferred holders must be made before common stock dividends can be paid. Preferred stocks usually do not have voting rights.

Principal: The original investment.

Real Estate Investment Trust (REIT): A corporation or trust that uses the pooled capital of many investors to purchase and manage income property (equity REIT) and/or mortgage loans (mortgage REIT). REITs are traded on major exchanges just like stocks. They are also granted special tax considerations. REITs offer several benefits over actually owning properties. First, they are highly liquid, unlike traditional real estate. Second, REITs enable sharing in nonresidential properties as well, such as hotels, malls, and other commercial or industrial properties. Third, there's no minimum investment with REITs. REITs do not necessarily increase and decrease in value along with the broader market. However, they pay yields in the form of dividends no matter how the shares perform. REITs can be valued based upon fundamental measures, similar to the valuation of stocks, but different numbers tend to be important for REITs than for stocks.

Record Date: The date on which a shareholder must officially own a stock's shares in order to receive a company's declared dividend or, among other things, to vote on company issues.

Return of Capital: A distribution of cash resulting from depreciation tax savings, the sale of a capital asset or securities, or any other transaction unrelated to retained earnings.

Total Return: An investment's annual return based on appreciation and dividends or interest.

Unit Investment Trust (UIT): A US investment company offering a fixed (unmanaged) portfolio of securities having a definite life. UITs are assembled by a sponsor and sold through brokers to investors.

INDEX